GOD

An Obituary

Peter Heinegg

Hamilton Books
A member of
The Rowman & Littlefield Publishing Group
Lanham · Boulder · New York · Toronto · Plymouth, UK

Copyright © 2009 by
Hamilton Books
4501 Forbes Boulevard
Suite 200
Lanham, Maryland 20706
Hamilton Books Acquisitions Department (301) 459-3366

Estover Road
Plymouth PL6 7PY
United Kingdom

All rights reserved
Printed in the United States of America
British Library Cataloging in Publication Information Available

Library of Congress Control Number: 2009928752
ISBN-13: 978-0-7618-4712-0 (paperback : alk. paper)
ISBN-10: 0-7618-4712-X (paperback : alk. paper)
eISBN-13: 978-0-7618-4713-7
eISBN-10: 0-7618-4713-8

™ The paper used in this publication meets the minimum
requirements of American National Standard for Information
Sciences—Permanence of Paper for Printed Library Materials,
ANSI Z39.48-1992

To my brothers and sisters:
Paul, Thomas, Louise, Andrew,
Philip, John, Maria, Cathy, James

Contents

Acknowledgments		vii
Introduction		ix
Chapter One	Is God *Really* Dead?	1
Chapter Two	The Bible: Tainted Evidence for God	9
Chapter Three	Will the Real God Please Stand Up?	17
Chapter Four	God-Talk: The Wonderful World of Make-Believe	23
Chapter Five	Beating a Dead God	29
Chapter Six	Don't Do as God Says—or as He Does	35
Chapter Seven	God is Spirit—But What's That?	43
Chapter Eight	God Falling Short? Extrapolate, Extrapolate!	49
Chapter Nine	Holy Wars: God's Olympics	55
Chapter Ten	God the Father—and the Perils of Permanent Puerility	65
Chapter Eleven	Your God's Too Big	71
Chapter Twelve	God the Bully: Sic Semper Tyrannis	77
Chapter Thirteen	Divine Megalomania—It's Catching	83
Chapter Fourteen	God Abuses Animals	89
Chapter Fifteen	God is So Sexy	95
Chapter Sixteen	The Death of Allah: A Consummation Devoutly to be Wished	103
Chapter Seventeen	Jews Dispense with God—and You Can Too	109
Chapter Eighteen	A Humorless God	115
Chapter Nineteen	God Closes the Deal	121
Conclusion	The Future of God	129
About the Author		133

Acknowledgments

I wish to thank Penguin Books for permission to quote from N.J Dawood's translation of *The Koran*, 50th anniversary edition, 2006. Bible citations, unless otherwise indicated, are from the King James Version. All other translations, unless otherwise indicated, are by myself.

As for death among such [divine] beings, I have heard the words of a man who was not a fool nor an impostor . . . [namely] Epitherses, who lived in our town and was my teacher in grammar. He said that once upon a time in making a voyage to Italy he embarked on a ship carrying freight and many passengers. It was already evening when, near the Echinades Islands, the wind dropped, and the ship drifted near Paxi. Almost everybody was awake, and a good many had not finished their after-dinner wine. Suddenly from the island of Paxi was heard the voice of someone loudly calling Thamus, so that all were amazed. Thamus was an Egyptian pilot, not known by name even to many on board. Twice he was called and made no reply, but the third time he answered; and the caller, raising his voice, said, "When you come opposite to Palodes, announce that Great Pan is dead." On hearing this, all, said Epitherses, were astounded and reasoned among themselves whether it were better to carry out the order or to refuse to meddle and let the matter go. Under the circumstances Thamus made up his mind that if there should be a breeze, he would sail past and keep quiet, but with no wind and a smooth sea about the place he would announce what he had heard. So, when he came opposite Palodes, and there was neither wind nor wave, Thamus from the stern, looking toward the land, said the words as he had heard them: "Great Pan is dead." Even before he had finished there was a great cry of lamentation, not of one person, but of many, mingled with exclamations of amazement.

—Plutarch, *Moralia* 5, 17, tr. F. C. Babbitt

Introduction

> A peculiar chill of horror, a mysterious sense of awe forbids us to write any further today. Our breast is full of a dreadful pity—old Jehovah himself is preparing for death. We have known him so well, from his cradle onwards, back in Egypt where he was brought up amongst divine calves, crocodiles, sacred onions, ibises, and cats. —We have seen him, as he bade farewell to these playthings of his childhood and the obelisks and sphinxes of his native Nile valley, became a little god-king in Palestine, with a poor nation of shepherds, and settled down in his own temple-palace. We saw him later on, when he came into contact with Assyrian-Babylonian civilization, and laid aside his all-too-human passions, no longer just spewing out rage and revenge, or at least no longer instantly hurling thunderbolts down at every bit of despicable behavior. —We saw him emigrate to Rome, the imperial city, where he renounced all national prejudices and proclaimed the heavenly equality of all peoples, and with the use of such smooth phrases formed the opposition party against old Jupiter, and intrigued for so long until he took complete control, and from atop the Capitol ruled the city and the world, *urbem et orbem*. —We saw how he became more and more spiritualized, how softly and blissfully he whimpered, how be became an amiable Father, a generic Friend to Man, a Contributor to World Happiness, a Philanthropist—but none of it could save him. —Can't you hear those little bells tinkling? Down on your knees. —They're bringing the sacraments to a dying God.
>
> —Heinrich Heine, *On the History of Religion and Philosophy in Germany* (1834-5)

The title of this book is a spin-off of Jack Miles's *God: A Biography* (1995). Miles ends his fine survey of God's checkered career in the Hebrew Bible by calling the deity "that divided original" (divided, that is, between omnipotence over us and solicitude for us), "whose divided image we remain. His is the restless breathing we still hear in our sleep." My not-exactly-novel point here is that God, in fact, has stopped breathing, that no amount of artificial respiration can bring him back, and that any breathing we might still hear is our own. The date of God's demise may be as unspecifiable as his date of birth; but that death is nonetheless real, and we need to write and talk (more) about it.

Freud taught us that many features of our dreams are overdetermined; and nowhere is this truer than with God, who died from a complex syndrome of ailments, most of which this book will explore, at least briefly. Insofar as God is/was a dreamed-up concept, he died of massive inconsistencies and incoherence. The more reasons theologians concoted to explain how God transcends reason and sense experience—somehow without contradicting them—the more leaks their arguments sprang. God died because people found and began relying on more ready-to-hand accounts for how things work. For example, empires fall because of political and economic troubles, not because God punishes rulers and nations for idolatry and other sins. Mortality comes from our genes, not from some inherited Adamic curse.

God died because erstwhile believers learned they didn't need him to live morally (in fact, many of God's laws, such as those promoting slavery and misogyny, were exposed as indefensible). God died because the proofs of his existence and power were so shaky. He died because of the catastrophic perceived flaws in his "creation" and management of the world. When measured by his actual performance, as opposed to what might have been (except, the God-talkers assure us, for the intractability of crude matter or the well-deserved consequences of the Fall), God always fell short.

God died, in other words, because he failed to deliver. The sacred scriptures of Jews, Christians, and Muslims promise (and threaten) way too much; and over time believers, at least the more alert ones, began to realize that the various divinely indited scenarios hadn't yet and wouldn't ever come true. In general, the more carefully one reads the Bible and the Qur'an, the worse they look. God notoriously abandoned the Jews, but he didn't do much better with the Christians and the Muslims (if they ever bothered to do the math, they would have figured that out—and many did). God died because the once majestic figure of Yahweh, or his younger brother Allah, struck more and more people as a repellent bully. He died because of the monstrous crimes committed by persons claiming to enjoy a special intimacy with him and to be acting on his authority.

(This might seem unfair, but God never says anything of importance to humans except through his representatives; and so we have the right to judge him by the company he keeps—unless those anointed, canonized mouthpieces were flat-out lying when they said they met him.) God died because he was insensitive to animals and the natural world (imagine drowning all the creatures in a gigantic zoo just because their keepers had gotten out of line); and some people, e.g., vegetarians, started showing more care for his creatures than he did.

God died because millions of people tried and failed to relate to him. He was, as some theologians like to say, "totally Other," which is a terrible basis for friendship. Putting it a different way, God is pure spirit (no body, no gender, no history, no time or place or limitations) ; and how many of us have ever met a spirit? Paradoxically, despite his stellar talents and intelligence, God died because he bored people; he kept repeating himself; he had no sense of humor, and didn't play well with others. Unlike the pronouncements of the theologians, all the foregoing antitheistic claims can be rationally and empirically defended, and they will be, in the pages that follow.

One subject I won't much bother about in this book is the well-worn philosophical arguments for God's existence, such as Thomas Aquinas's Five Ways (Unmoved Mover, First Cause, Contingency-Necessity, Degrees of Perfection, and Final Causality). The problem with all such arguments—apart from their being untrue—is that even if you find them convincing, they don't get you very far. The distance separating an Unmoved Mover (whatever *that* is) and the "juicy" God of Abraham, Isaac, Jacob, Jesus, and Muhammad is all but infinite. What Pascal called "the God of the philosophers" is of little interest, except as a floor routine for dogmatizing gymnasts—and the odd believer looking to add some intellectual respectability to his or her mythic creed, the way baby-boomers used to buy the *Encyclopedia Britannica* or *The World Book* for their dens. The God that matters and the God whose obituary needs to be written is the old familiar scriptural Super-Star.

I should add, for purposes of full disclosure, that I myself am a former professional theist. I was born into a devoutly Catholic family (ten children!), went to Catholic schools in New York (including Fordham University), and began attending daily mass when I was thirteen. I spent seven years (1959-1966) in the Jesuit order; and well into my twenties I was intent on becoming a celibate Catholic priest. Fate (and sanity) decided otherwise. In my old age I have become as passionately anti-religious as I was pious in my youth. I've also taught and written about the Bible for almost four decades. None of this gives my book any magical cachet of credibility; but I can say that I've been there and done that. The harsh criticism that I will now dish out—not for the first time, cf. my *Good God! (And Other Follies): Essays on Religion* (2007)—is based on long experience.

Speaking of that experience, especially the juvenile and adolescent parts (up to the point when, at age twenty-four, I left the seminary and most of my religious life behind), let me use it to take a brief shot at answering the one question about God that most baffles people who have never believed: How do you get started? Whence comes that weird conviction or fantasy that you're in contact with the most uncanny of all uncanny Beings? Whence all the thrills and chills flooding believers' sensoria when they "feel the Spirit" or leap to their feet for the Hallelujah Chorus?

I take it for granted that, as mentioned, practically no one believes in God because of arguments, cosmological, ontological, teleological, or otherwise. Something has to *happen* (barring the not-trivial number of religious liars and bullshitters who just like to hear themselves talk). Unfortunately, neither I nor anyone else can remember when we were first told about God; but I'm guessing that the earliest stages of the process resemble the familiar moment in childhood when someone tells you that if you put a conch to your ear, you can hear the ocean. And, by God, you can—or something that sounds like the ocean! (Only later, often much later, do you learn that it's just ambient noise.) Similarly, you get taken to some kind of service in church or synagogue when you're young, having been prepped to sense that you'll be coming (somehow, as they say) into the presence of a mysterious force called God. Once transported into this extraordinary environment—utterly unlike a house, an apartment, a store, a street, all the places you know—you will, perforce, see and hear all sorts of unusual things, not least of all the strenuous expressions on the faces of adults and the unctuous utterances of a professional God-talker. (If you're a Catholic, as I was, you'll get an extra helping of sensory impressions from the statuary, stained glass windows, and frescoes, whose likely garishness won't bother you in the least.)

So, now you're launched: God at this point is the invisible source of the vague, but intriguing sensations that seem to emanate from inside the sacred building (and, once you train yourself to concentrate on them, from outside as well). Autosuggestion (with a hint of autoeroticism?)

Introduction xiii

takes care of the rest. You build enough synaptic connections, call the whole grid God, talk to it, plead with it, meditate on it; and eventually you (may) feel the wires humming. Only the schizophrenic or "spiritually gifted" ever hear God talking back to them (cf. William James's description of George Fox, the founder of the Quakers, as a "détraqué of the deepest dye"); but that's where the Bible and Qur'an come in. While reading or recalling the inspired "word of God," you can imagine—some devotees have a special knack for this—that God himself is speaking to you through one or more of his scriptural spokesmen. (See Chapter Two, "The Bible: Tainted Evidence For God.") And you're off.

Once this syndrome is in place, it gets reinforced by formal religious education (of which I had twenty, count 'em, twenty years' worth). Pre-indoctrinated children are handed over to adult propagandists who deepen their charges' faith through catechism, Talmud Torah, Sunday school and its various equivalents, confraternity classes, religious summer camps, liturgies, home rituals, parental example and exhortation, books, movies, etc.

Another huge factor here is the general cultural mindset, shaping and stuffing young brains long before they're conscious of it (which explains why Saudi Arabia, which has twice the population of Sweden, has far fewer atheists). These days faith is anachronistically alive and well in America, while open unbelief is still rare, as the polls and surveys continue to show. (It was even rarer in the 1940s and '50s, when I was growing up.) But it's spreading; and if the course of European history is any guide, we should expect it to become more respectable, if not prevalent, as time goes on. Who knows, maybe one day Americans will give as much credence to evolution as they now give to the Virgin birth. Still, as long as the country keeps fueling its religious hothouses (red states, mega-churches, Mormon temples, Christian colleges, Evangelical homeschools, prayer meetings, etc.), the weird flowers of godliness will continue to, er, blossom in the land of the dim and the home of the dumb.

Peter Heinegg
Schenectady, NY

Chapter One

Is God *Really* Dead?

Haven't you heard about the madman who kindled a lantern one bright morning, ran to the marketplace, and wouldn't stop crying out, "I'm looking for God! I'm looking for God!" Since, as it happened, many of the bystanders didn't believe in God, that stirred up gales of laughter. "Oh, did he get lost?" asked one. "Did he go astray, like a child?" asked another. "Or is he hiding? Is he afraid of us? Has he gone off to sea? Emigrated?" they shouted, and all laughed at once.

The madman sprang into their midst and riveted them with his look. "Where has God gone?" he cried. "I shall tell you. We killed him—you and I. We are his murderers. But how did we do it? How did we manage to drink up the sea? Who gave us the sponge to wipe away the entire horizon? What did we do when we unchained this earth from its sun? Where is it headed now? Where are *we* headed now? Away from all suns? Aren't we continuously plunging backwards, sidewards, forwards, in all directions? Is there still an up and a down? Aren't we wandering through an infinite nothingness? Isn't the emptiness of space breathing in our faces? Hasn't it gotten colder? Isn't night and more night coming on all the tme? Don't we have to light lanterns in the morning? Don't we hear any sounds from the gravediggers burying God? Don't we notice any smell from God's decaying—Gods rot away too. God is dead. God remains dead. And we have killed him. How can we, the murderers of all murderers, ever console ourselves? The holiest and mightiest thing that the world ever possessed has bled to death beneath our knives. Who will wash this blood off us? What sort of water shall we use to purify ourselves? What days of atonement, what sacred games shall we have to institute? Isn't this deed too great for us? Wouldn't we have to become gods to seem worthy of it? There never has been a greater deed—and anyone born after it will be part, thanks to this deed, of a history loftier than any previous history ever was."

Here the madman fell silent and looked again at his listeners. They too fell silent and looked at him, disconcerted. Finally he threw his lantern down on the ground, where it shattered and went out. "I've come too soon," he said. "It isn't time yet. This enormous event is still underway and in motion. It hasn't yet reached the ears of men and women. Lightning and thunder need time, the light of the stars needs time, deeds need time, after they've been done, to be seen and heard. This deed is still further away from them than the farthest constellations—and yet they have done it themselves."—The story goes on to relate that on that same day the madman made his way into various churches and there intoned his eternal requiem to God. When they led him outside and took him to task for this, he kept giving the same answer: "Well, what are these churches, then, if not the tombs and gravestones of God?"

—Nietzsche, *The Gay Science*, 125

The scene has been endlessly revisited, the story keeps getting retold. Collegiate wits used to scrawl "God is dead, signed Nietzsche—Nietzsche is dead, signed God" in bathroom cubicles and on subway walls. In the 1970s and '80s a curious school of "death-of-God theologians" (Yahweh is gone, but not forgotten) came and went. And God (not to mention Allah) has been very much among the undead in America since the rise of the Evangelicals in the Reagan years. But Nietzsche was still brilliantly right back in 1882 when he first published *The Gay Science*.

First of all, God is not simply or primarily dead—he has been murdered. He was a cultural creation to begin with, and his creators killed him off—for all sorts of reasons, rage, disgust, disappointment, boredom, restlessness, and sometimes just by accident or for a joke, as when the thirteen-year-old Mary McCarthy (in *Memories of a Catholic Girlhood*, 1957) pretended to have a crisis of faith just to make herself more interesting to her confessor, and then discovered after talking it over that she actually didn't believe in God after all.

As the madman emphatically reminds us, this is a very big deal. Note that his audience isn't made up of scandalized churchgoers, but of jaded atheists who can't see what the fuss is all about (these days their equivalent might be academics sipping their coffee in the faculty lounge).

In mocking the problem of God's permanent absence, they echo Elijah mocking the priests of Baal in 1 Kings 18.27 ("Cry aloud, for he is a god; either he is musing, or he has gone aside [i.e., to relieve himself], or he is on a journey, or perhaps he is asleep and must be awakened," RSV). In other words, to the casual 19th century unbeliever God was a ridiculous, non-existing popular idol, just as Baal was to a 9th century BCE Israelite prophet.

But they were wrong; and this happens to be a point that contemporary theists, agnostics, and atheists can agree on: Whatever else God may in reality *be*, "he" is also and in various ways a cultural construct. His transcendent "reality" always has to be mediated to us earthbound, sense-addicted mortals through coarse-grained images. Thus, God is presented and understood as a hyper-masculine monarch, a tender buddy, a ruthless enforcer of a primitive ethical code, or a mostly silent Answer-Man (a default explanation for all not-yet-understood events in nature). Well, good riddance, many (liberal) Jews and Christians would say to such bad old ideas.

Beyond that, God-friendly thinkers might concede that the most of the great cultural forces of modernity, in both the arts and the sciences, have arisen and gone on without benefit of clergy. Like Pierre Simon de Laplace, the leading lights of the contemporary world haven't seen the need for any theistic hypotheses. And so, they and their countless aiders and abettors have killed God in both their public and private lives.

In this vein, one recalls Georg Lukacs's dictum that the novel is the epic of a world without God. Accordingly, the modest-sized guild of novelists (who didn't get busy till the 18th century) and the vast army of novel-readers inhabit a universe from which God gets banished as a matter of course, not just as an agent, but even as a spectator. Again, this isn't a matter of "ultimate reality" (whatever that is), but of mass consciousness. God is, by and large, missing from the "secular city" and its doings, perhaps relegated to the canonical hour-a-week of worship in some tame sacred space, but otherwise unavailable. It's not like Homer, where the gods, most of them in mufti, show up everywhere.

Along with this silence comes sterility: The theistic traditions have produced nothing of real interest for many decades now, neither in the pseudo-science of God-talk (theology), nor in the philosophical spill-over from it, nor in the arts. Secularists rule. The most thriving, in fact positively booming, branch of theism is without question Islam; and who was the last Islamic theologian or thinker to say anything of importance to anyone except sociologists and historians of Islam itself? The brilliant-but-bygone "glories of Islam" belong in a coffee-table book or a tourist's itinerary (from Cordova to Istanbul to Isfahan to Agra), not in the contemporary marketplace of ideas. (Could there be a causal link between the deep religiosity of Muslims and the utter backwardness of their economic, political, and intellectual life?)

So, to oversimplify—but not by much—God is dead in the minds of the people who matter. To be sure, he continues to exist in the heads of the devout (the only place he ever did exist); but, given all the other bad ideas that do and will survive and thrive there (e.g., mythical auto-intoxication, tribal chauvinism, sexism, speciesism, homophobia, etc.), that's not a recommendation. While the biblical prophets and Muhammad in the Qur'an are sadly deficient in humor (see Chapter Eighteen, "A Humorless God"), they never stop pouring ridicule over idols and idolaters (for example in Isaiah 44). But what is Yahweh-Allah, if not a purely human concept, "made of hands"? Banning images of wood and stone won't remove all the childish images stockpiled in believers' brains. But once you realize just how infantile those images are, you can proceed directly to God's funeral.

As Freud wrote in *The Future of An Illusion:* "The gods still have their threefold assignment: they have to drive out the terrors of nature, to reconcile human beings to the cruelty of fate, especially as seen in death, and to compensate them for the sufferings and deprivations imposed on them by life together in civilization." The classic secular response to this is: But of course—how could you *not* suspect that the Big-Daddy-in-the-Sky dreams or deliriums of religion were made up, subconsciously or otherwise, to allay our fears and provide (bogus) security in an insecure cosmos?

The classic believing response is: Well, just because a story has a happy ending doesn't mean it *has* to be false—maybe we *do* have a loving heavenly Father. You never know. (Actually, that's the honest believing response. The more typical dishonest one is to pretend that the propositions of faith are as solid as the periodic table of the elements, just not subject, like this-worldly statements, to challenge and falsification. As the churchy old mantra used to intone: For those who believe no explanation is necessary; for those who do not believe, no explanation is possible. (So all you skeptics just shut up.)

Eventually, the whole issue comes down, as Freud argued, to growing up and getting rid of the Old Man (see Chapter Ten, "God the Father—and the Perils of Permanent Puerility"). If that sounds too Oedipal, maybe the operative image shouldn't be slaying the tyrannical Father (a 19th century affair, since back then papas, especially in Mitteleuropa, those stern, bearded, frock-coated, cigar-smoking ,etc. patriarchs, had more power than they do now) so much as euthanizing the Alzheimer's patient, formalizing a process that for all intents and purposes is already over. Of course, even pulling the plug on a moribund God or giving him an merciful overdose of morphine, is still a big step, as Nietzsche's madman warned.

Speaking of patients *in extremis*, there's a suggestive analogy to be drawn between the history of medicine and the laughable pseudo-science of theology. Americans today are devout believers in the all-but-miraculous powers of medical science, even as medieval Catholics looked to theology as the "queen of the sciences." But then, David Wootton reminds us in *Bad Medicine: Doctors Doing Harm Since Hippocrates* (2006), for well over two millennia physicians were a deadly threat to their patients' health, thanks to all the bloodletting, emetics, purgatives, and cauteries they so gleefully administered, thanks to the often lethal surgery, the iatrogenic diseases (e.g., puerperal fever), and the incredible ignorance of these pseudo-experts on the human body. It wasn't until around 1930 that going to the doctor was a better bet for your health than staying at home and letting nature take its course. And for something under two millennia (if we start with St. Paul) theologians have been blindly misunderstanding the universe, misdiagnosing the troubles of humanity, and mistreating their gullible followers.

Early physicians conjured up bogus entities—humors, miasmas, internally wandering wombs—and fabricated systems to deal with them. Theologians invented God, angels, and demons, and built mind-boggling schemata of sin, guilt, redemption, revelation, sacred history, and so forth. No real evidence was ever supplied for any of this; and, amazingly, none was demanded. The key to whatever success old-time medicine enjoyed was, Wootton shows, the placebo effect: Patients who believed the nonsense fed them by doctors, who were of course revered figures, got a jolt of confidence that helped release pain-killing endorphins and other self-healing bodily reponses. Priests and clergymen no doubt induced feelings of comfort and relief in their congregations—having first prompted the prerequisite misery, fear of punishent, hope for forgiveness, fantasies of salvation and damnation, etc.—through a similar mechanism.

Wootton quotes a disillusioned 18th century physician, William Taplin, who satirized the medical con game in *Aesculapian Labyrinth* (1789), which advised doctors that whilst visiting patients they should

> take care to *look* wisdom in every feature: speak but little, and let it be impossible *that little* should be understood; let every hint, every *shrug* be carefully calculated to give the hearers a wonderful opinion of your learning and experience. —In your *half-heard* and mysterious conversation with your *medical inferior* [the apothecary], do not forget to drop a few observations upon—"the animal economy— . . . "the non naturals"—"stricture upon the parts" . . . and all those *technical traps* that fascinate the hearers, and render the patient yours ad libitum. (*Bad Medicine,* p. 296, emphases in original)

The theological equivalents are obvious: begowned, Roman-collared, grandly titled reverends (lit. = "to-be-feared-ones") spouting their arcane rigmarole about "original sin," "atonement," "incarnation," "grace," "holiness," and so on. Their well-primed audience is, predictably, awed, moved, and consoled. (Though what if one could sue for religious malpractice—lives ruined or spoiled by theological quackery?) People must have been deriving *some* mental benefits from religion; or the whole business would have collapsed by now. Not all depressed Christians are hypochondriacs; and not all supposed "cures" are frauds.

Still, all bad things must come to an end. In the face of dogged resistance from the medical profession (Molière's Drs. Diafoirus), science began to win out over pseduo-scientific abracadabra. Material reality—as in the germ theory of disease, the use of antiseptics, water filtration, vaccinations, etc.—triumphed over mumb-jumbo. Wootton, along with other scholars, traces the beginning of modern, i.e., real, medicine back to Joseph Lister and Louis Pasteur The 19th century likewise saw traditional religion take a number of devastating hits, as historians (Renan), Bible scholars (Wellhausen), archeologists (Petrie et al.), psychologists (Nietzsche!), sociologists (Durkheim), philosophers (from Mill to Marx and beyond), and, yes, theologians (David Strauss) analyzed and dissolved cherished myths.

Unfortunately, whereas quackery suffered devastating debacles and has almost disappeared, theism, mortally wounded as it is, continues to prevail in the less enlightened regions of the planet and among the less educated strata of the population. No wonder there, for the turbid origins of religion predate the rise of Judaism, Christianity, and Islam; and, when cornered, apologists for theism take refuge in the trackless Waziristan of the supernatural, which is by definition invulnerable to all empirical probes. There's no telling how long theistic follies may last (doctors were still bleeding the sick in 1870); but, as with modern medical technology, the testimony of cured and recovering believers should go a long way to establishing that life is plainly, pragmatically better without the hocus-pocus of religion.

So then, *is* God really dead? Inevitably, yes and no. Like unicorns, basilisks, centaurs, mermaids, werwolves, cockatrices, griffons, rocs, heffalumps, and flying monkeys, God is a creature of fantasy and, as such, "he" has been wiped out by our knowledge of reality. But any creature of fantasy can be resurrected and kept alive by gullible imaginations. However, while persistent reports of, say, the Loch Ness Monster have to face a skeptical enfilade from journalists and scientists, accounts of people "finding" Jesus or even just "searching for God" must be treated with poker-faced respect. To be looking for God earns you brownie points in modernity: I'm a seeker! That shows a delicate sensibility, an open mind, as opposed to the fat-headed (and often fat-assed) complacency of the "God Said It, I Believe It, That Settles It" crowd. But believers of all stripes, from agonizing Kierkegaardians to attitudinizing televangelists, are simply wrong. And they need to be called out on it—which is what this book attempts to do.

Chapter Two

The Bible: Tainted Evidence for God

> And God said unto Moses, "I AM THAT I AM": and he said, "Thus shalt Thou say unto the children of Israel, "I AM hath sent me unto you." And God said moreover unto Moses, "Thus shalt thou say unto the children of Israel, 'The LORD God of your fathers, the God of Abraham, the God of Isaac, and the God of Jacob, hath sent me unto you; this is my name forever.'"
>
> —Exodus 3.14-15

> Jesus said unto them, "Verily, verily, I say unto you, before Abraham was, I am."
>
> —John 8.58

People know about, and believe in, God because other people have talked them into it. Those people, in turn, have heard about God from other people (mostly older ones), in a theological daisy chain spinning back to the cave men. At some point these accounts get collected and canonized as Holy Writ—and then the trouble really begins. Studying the Bible is supposed to promote faith; but the opposite is true, as any fair-minded reading of it—such as the one that follows—will show.

After a brief, but spectacular, debut as the Creator of the world (or Sculptor of Chaos), Yahweh settles into his far more crucial role as tribal leader, the God of the Hebrews-Israelites-Jews. But even before that fateful transition, there are some worrisome features in his profile. To begin with, we have his selfish, mean-spirited forbidding, first the tree of the knowledge of good and evil (were humans to remain moral infants?), then the tree of life (why not spread the wealth?) Literary critics are free to celebrate the "Fall" as a pregnant meditation on the mixed blessings of consciousness (some even see it as a feminist mythologem, with Eve leading the human race to self-awareness). But the text is harsh, with its out-of-nowhere unleashing of the curses on Adam and especially Eve (lifelong servitude to her husband) . Even worse, perhaps, is that ominous culminating anacoluthon: "And now, lest he put forth his hand, and take also of the tree of life, and eat, and live forever . . ." The very thought of humans living forever grosses God out (he changed his mind on that later, coincidentally after the Jews came into contact with cultures, in Persia and Greece, that believed in life after death, and at a time when a long series of persecutions and political disasters made it all but impossible to believe that justice, divine or otherwise, could be had in the here and now.)

Then comes the monstrous massacre of the Flood, which even YHWH realizes was overkill, as he promises never to do it again. The nature of the LORD (later manifested in his simmering jealousy of other gods) comes through one last time before the emergence of the Hebrews when he gets into a tizzy over the Tower of Babel: "Behold the people is one, and they have all one language: and this they begin to do: and now nothing will be restrained from them, which they have imagined to do. Go to, let us go down, and there confound their language, that they may not understand one another's speech" (Genesis 11.6). That'll show 'em— as if God had nothing better to do with his time than cause deadly linguistic-social disruption .

Starting in chapter 12 of Genesis, the LORD's unexplained choice of, and continued favoritism to, Abraham, lays the foundation for a mostly idyllic series of tales—apart from the awful Binding of Isaac. It's surprising to see the Maker of the Universe take up the much narrower specialty of wonder-working gynecologist for the three sterile matriarchs, Sarah, Rebekah, and Rachel (there's no male infertility in the Bible); but that's all part of his grand geopolitical design. In any case, by the end of Genesis it's clear that although Yahweh hasn't yet given a proper definition of himself (and won't until the New Testament), he views and rules the world from an androcentric throne.

God speaks almost exclusively to males. He has no problem with polygamy, and he shows a keen interest in "seed" (he slays Onan for spilling his precious semen outside Tamar's vagina, Gen. 38.9). Fabulously prolific himself, he passes on that gift to, of all people, the aged

Abraham: "Look now towards heaven, and tell the stars, if thou be able to number them so shall thy seed be" (Gen. 15.5).

By the time the Book of Exodus opens, God's aggressive natalism has raised a childless (apart from the irrelevant Ishmael) centenarian and his post-menopausal wife to the level of progenitors of ca. 3,000,000 Israelites (judging from the 600,000-man army that crosses the Red Sea and marches into Sinai, Ex. 12.37). Curiously, as soon as the Hebrews are delivered into the vestibule to the Promised land, relations between them and the LORD sour, and for the rest of biblical history they improve only for brief intervals. Aaron leads the blasphemous apostasy of the golden calf, which makes Yahweh, not for the last time, feel like nuking his "stiff-necked people" and starting over again from scratch. Moses talks him out of it, of course; but then he launches a bloody sectarian purge that costs 3,000 lives.

Eventually, the LORD gets so fed up with his people (and with Moses himself, who—in what Freud thought might be a masturbation-fantasy— whacks a rock with his staff and bids it spew forth water instead of simply *telling* it to spout, as God had bidden him) that he condemns the entire original Exodus generation to die in the wilderness, sparing only Caleb and Joshua.

And so it goes: after conquering Canaan, the Israelites spend about four hundred years under the wild and crazy Judges, constantly succumbing to the lure of the Baals and being bloodily punished for it by the Lord. Saul's kingship ends in military disaster. The eras of David and Solomon see only mixed success, and the great bulk of the kings who follow them are despicable failures. The northern kingdom (the Ten Lost Tribes) gets annihilated by God with help from the Assyrians in 722 B.C.E. The southern kingdom is overwhelmed by the (God-appointed) Babyonians in 586 B.C.E. and essentially doesn't come back until 1948, after which its fortunes continue to be shaky.

Again, apart from some golden moments, like the early reign of David or the legendary days of Solomon (when "Judah and Israel dwelt safely, every man under his vine and under his fig tree, from Dan even to Beersheba" 1 Kings 4.25), most of the time God is in varying states of apoplectic rage and disgust with his people, who for their part are forever backsliding and breaking the covenant. (And we can't put too much faith in that sunny piece of propaganda about Solomon, because the same text also claims that his sway extended all the way to the Euphrates, which is palpable nonsense.) Major portions of the Bible might be fairly summarized as "God kvetches about his people—and his people kvetch back."

The whole top-down, yet topsy-turvy business seems to make very little sense. In what's known as the Deuteronomic principle God (speaking through Moses and all the other prophets) solemnly promises that if you do good (obey the law), you'll fare well. But anyone who looks out the window can see that this isn't how things work. (Jeremiah, in 12.1-4, and Job, passim, bring that discrepancy to the LORD's attention, but he doesn't—because he can't—clear up their cognitive dissonance).

In the early phase of his dealings with Israel, God performs all kinds of sensational favors for his people. This peaks (ha) with his giving Moses the law on Mount Sinai/Horeb, after which he tends to fade from the picture. It's true, he guides their supposedly genocidal campaign under Joshua against the Canaanites; but no sooner does the Book of Joshua wind up its triumphal parade than the Book of Judges reveals that Joshua was theo-propaganda: the Canaanites are still alive and kicking. Then the Philistines arrive on the scene, and the *Sitz im Leben* gets even messier.

So where is God in all this? Nowhere to be seen: Isaiah crows about the return from exile in 538 B.C.E., but even he has to admit that it was Cyrus who, historically speaking, pushed the levers of power. In any case, the Persians passed the Jews on to the Greeks, who passed them on to the Romans, who passed them on to the Arabs, who passed them on to the Turks, who passed them on to the Brits, who gave up in disgust. Some sacred history. By the time of the Book of Esther, with its blood-drenched counter-pogroms (75,810 anti-Semites slain), God isn't mentioned once: He's done his job and can go off into discreet retirement. The Jews have themselves and Judaism (or Yiddishkeit) which apparently is all they need. (See Chapter Seventeen, "Jews Dispense with God—And You Can Too.")

But wait, isn't religion first and foremost about God? Not really. It was an unbelieving Jew, Émile Durkheim, who showed, in *The Elementary Structures of Religious Life* (1912), that the focus of any religious community, or what he called "a church," was not the deity, but itself, which it celebrates and advances in creed, code, and cult. Note that, as mentioned, for almost the entire Hebrew Bible God's chosen people did *not* believe in an afterlife, so there was no way that dead believers could dwell with God or be rewarded or punished beyond the grave. ("What profit is there in my blood, when I go down to the pit?" asks the Psalmist, a little snottily, "Shall the dust praise thee?" Ps. 30.9) And hence religion in the end has far more to do with the crudities of communal solidarity (three cheers for us!) than with the refinements of piety ("selfless devotion"). And theomanic patriots from one country have a habit of declaring war on and slaughtering their opposite numbers elsewhere (see Chapter Nine, "Holy Wars: God's Olympics").

Christianity, as its rapid expansion showed, was a much easier religion to practice than Judaism. The onerous Halakhic requirements were stripped away, and a fat package of mouth-watering promises (and bone-chilling threats) added on: a proximate end of the world and eternal happiness with Jesus in the New Jerusalem. In the meantime there was unearned forgiveness (talk about a psychological boost!) for all sins and crimes by virtue of a murky substitutionary atonement (one judicial murder buys eternal life for everyone else), where the torture and crucifixion of Jesus appeases his implacable Father. Unlike the God of Judaism, who no longer spoke to earthlings from out of a cloud, and who hadn't worked any miracles since maybe the first Chanukah (165 BCE—and that one's not even in the Bible), the activist God of Christianity took on flesh, flew down to earth, cleaned everything up, and readied the world for take off. A major improvement—if only it were true.

But the much-vaunted Second Coming never came, and all the problems and contradictions from the Old Testament overflowed into the New. Insofar as God was transcendent, he was too much to handle; and we could make no sense of him. Insofar as he was "like us," he was just a glorified chum. Insofar as he was unlimited, he had no shape (a Great Galactic Glob). Insofar as he was limited (like a person, say, with gender and individual features), he was nothing out of the ordinary. Basically, he looked like one huge projection of ourselves: a master craftsman-cum-family doctor-cum-mighty warrior-cum-hyperactive legislator-cum-moralizing preacher-cum-jack-of-all-trades. What a man!

The more God talked (through his messengers) and showed us (through his punishments) about himself, the worse he looked. He kept sounding suspiciously like his prophet du jour: angry (someone has calculated that three-fourths of all prophetic oracles in the Bible are negative), indignant, sarcastic, consoling, whatever. And always *echt* masculine. God-as-Jesus bore a remarkable resemblance to a hot-headed young Jewish zealot, with all those over-the-top warnings and demands. (Christians never heed them, but they seem to like the radical *frisson* they get just from hearing them read out loud: "And if any man will sue thee at the law, and take away thy coat, let him have thy cloak also," Mt. 5.40—in überlitigious America? Are you putting me on?)

Maybe that was it: Jews and Christians both (and Muslims too) are willing to swallow all the nonsensicalities imaginable in exchange for the blissed-out rush of believing that they're in touch with Someone in the Great Somewhere. And, in a strange sort of harking back to pre-Gutenberg days, when both books and literacy were rare, believers seem to be naively overawed by the fact that all the supposed divine dictates are *printed* (!), *in black and white*(!), and, often enough, *in leather-bound volumes* (!) *with gilt pages* (!) *and a shiny red ribbon book mark*(!) Add to that the solemn archaic diction ("O house of Jacob, come ye,. And let us walk in the light of the LORD"), exotic names (Kibroth-hattaavah. Maher-shalal-hash-baz, the angel of the church of the Laodiceans), the obscure splendor and splendid obscurity of so many passages ("When ye therefore shall see the abomination of desolation, spoken of by Daniel the prophet, stand in the holy place [whoso readeth, let him understand], then let them which be in Judea flee into the mountains," Matthew 24.15), and the sheer heft of the Bible (ca. 2,000 pages, depending on the edition, with the Apocrypha, maps, and notes); and it's no surprise that believers, both the minority who read the Bible and the majority who don't, should feel at least a faint shudder of awe at the numinous Word of God. 'Tain't nuthin' like it.

Except that, as even a semi-reflective reading of it will show, it's *not* the Word of God—or else God is an enormous moral and intellectual disappointment: a capricious, suspicious, contentious, pretentious, censorious, vainglorious Customer one doesn't feel drawn to become better acquainted with. One can say of the Bible what Samuel Johnson said of that grand Baroque take on it, *Paradise Lost*: no man ever wished it longer.

Yes, God's ventriloquists are often great poets; but there are also long stretches of the Bible (Exodus 36, Leviticus 13, Numbers 4, Joshua 19, Ezekiel 46, much of 1 Chronicles, etc.) so flat and tedious that any second-rate journalist or high school yearbook editor could easily dash off something better. The Bible, like its Author, leaves a lot to be desired. Of course, it's the height of political incorrectness to say that: Academic critics, for instance, rhapsodize about the literary subtlety and intricacy of Old Testament texts, without once asking the hard-boiled question: But is it *true*?

Of course not. It's a book, or rather a mini-library; and, like other libraries, it's full of fantasies, myths, lies, and errors, often woven inextricably together: superhighways through seas and rivers, raising and rising from the dead, magical killings of and by lions (Judges 14.6, 1 Kings 13.24), divine dietary laws (abolished when inconvenient, Acts 10.15), hares that chew the cud and menstrual blood that pollutes *everything*, the most acceptable sacrifices, from slaughtered and burnt cattle and sheep to an exsanguinated only-begotten Son, holy wars and unholy revenge, infinite blessings and infallible curses, ranting prophets and canting priests, whole heavenly-hellacious hoodoo of "divinity." Time to put it aside.

Chapter Three

Will the Real God Please Stand Up?

> Yet if oxen and lions had hands, and could paint with their hands,
> and fashion images, as men do,
> they would make the pictures and images of their gods
> in their own likeness;
> horses would make them like horses, oxen like oxen.
>
> Aethiopians make their gods black and snub-nosed;
> Thracians give theirs blue eyes and red hair.
>
> —Xenophanes (ca. 575-525 B.C.),
> fragments 15 and 16, tr. Arthur Fairbanks

> Droben in dem Sternenzelte,   Up there in the starry pavillion,
> Auf dem goldnen Herrscherstuhle,   On his golden Royal Throne
> Weltregierend, majestätisch,   World-controlling, so majestic
> Sitzt ein kolossaler Eisbär.   Sits a vast, gigantic polar bear.
>
> —Heinrich Heine, *Atta Troll*
> (a father bear is indoctrinating
> his young cub)

The bewildering, ludicrous multiplicity of deities in ancient and "primitive" religions has been a well-worn topic of both believing and unbelieving critics for millennia. Scoffers at popular religion, like Xenocrates or Lucretius or David Hume, enjoy pointing out the mutually exclusive ethnocentric and egocentric biases of God-lore. From elephantine Ganesh to simian Hanuman, from raptorish Horus to leonine Sekhmet, from gorgeous Aphrodite to gimpy Hephaestus, from humming-birdlike Huitzilopochtli to fierce feathered serpent Quetzalcoatl, from hammer-throwing Thor to trouble-making Loki, from the biblical bêtes noires Moloch, Astarte, and Baal to Muhammad's hated trio of goddesses Al-Lât, Al-'Uzzâ, and Manât, it does make a sensationally colorful, confusing, and silly show. How, one wonders, could their worshipers ever be talking about the same thing—unless that thing were, in the final analysis, themselves?

No one, of course, has flayed the chaotic grossness and dubious moral standards of pagan mythology more lustily than the monotheists. (And both Jews and Muslims have branded Christians as polytheists on account of the Trinity.) "All who make idols are nothing, and the things they delight in do not profit; their witnesses neither see nor know. And so they are put to shame. Who would fashion a god or cast an image that would do no good? Look, all its devotees shall be put to shame, the artisans too are merely human" (Isaiah 44. 9-10, RSV). Muhammad jibes at the devotees of goddesses: "When the birth of a girl is announced to any of them [the Meccans], his countenance darkens and he is filled with gloom. Would they ascribe to God females who adorn themselves with trinkets and are powerless in disputation?" (43:13). (Hm, sexist though the language is, doesn't he have a point here? Would Christians ever feel comfortable worshiping the Daughter of God?)

Unfortunately, even if we conceded every line in the monotheistic case, sticking points remain. First of all, why is Yahweh-Allah so furious at, and jealous of, the non-existent idols his spokesmen rail against? The obvious answer is that he's bothered by the competition. In fact, for much of biblical history before the 6th century B.C.E., the religion of ancient Israel wasn't monotheism, but henotheism. That is, Yahweh was the biggest and best of gods, but not the only one. And he had no qualms about admitting, in the text of the Ten Commandments for example, just how much the pagan gods got on his nerves. "For I the LORD thy God am a jealous God, visiting the iniquity of the fathers upon the children unto the third and fourth generation of them that hate me" (Exodus 20.5). No doubt the Israelites, in awe of the elaborate, sexy material culture of the Canaanites, with their priests and shrines and elaborate rites, just couldn't imagine that the gods of their neighbors were no more than phantasms. How not be impressed, for example, by the scene in 2 Kings 3.26-27, where Mesha, the desperate king of Moab, sacrifices his eldest son, the crown prince, on the city wall to gain victory from his gods over the besieging force of Israelites and Edomites—and the plan works!

This ticklish question—what exactly *are* the gods of the gentiles?—is resolved in principle by Second Isaiah (mid-6th century BCE) whose affirmation of the LORD's absolute uniqueness and unchallenged reality has been, as they say, the gold standard ever since. (Muhammad's fierce railing against idols seems to derive from the fact that he lived in a culture that took polytheism for granted. Constantly having to face insults, taunting, and worse from a hostile crowd is bound to try any prophet's patience.)

Having, with some difficulty, established that there was only one *real* God, Jews (and in time Christians) worked at sprucing up his image. After the Babylonian Exile (586-538 BCE) and the subsequent diaspora, Jews adopted a more liberal, "cosmopolitan" perspective, and so did Yahweh. In Deuteronomy 23.1 he told Moses that eunuchs couldn't be admitted "into the congregation of the LORD." But then in post-Exilic Isaiah 56.5 he announced that he would give Torah-abiding eunuchs "a place and a name better than of sons and daughters." In Deuteronomy 23.3 God banned Moabites from his congregation because of the grief they gave the Israelites fresh from the Exodus. And in the Books of Ezra and Nehemiah he lashed out fanatically against intermarriage with gentile women, demanding and getting instant mass divorces—something like a Unification Church wedding-fest in reverse.. But then in the Book of Ruth Yahweh blessed the entrance of a Moabitess not just into the congregation of Israel, but into the pedigree of King David, whose great-grandmother Ruth came from the hated land of Moab. Up until the first century CE Yahweh was a big fan of bloody animal sacrifices. But then, by a sort of inspired accident, the temple of Jerusalem got destroyed by the Romans in 70 CE; and the LORD lost his taste for that blessed butchery. The Jews, most of them, never looked back.

Beyond all that, Christians made God still more user-friendly by scrapping most of his more bothersome rules (circumcision, kashrut, eruv, tefillin, etc.) and stressing (sometimes) his mercy and forgiveness. Actually, Jews had already taken steps in the same direction, for example in the Book of Jonah, where Yahweh shows a broadminded concern for the fate of the Assyrians (whose name was mud since they had destroyed the Northern Kingdom of Israel in 722 BCE and scattered the Ten Lost Tribes to the four winds). God had always been a human artifact; and nowhere was this more palpable than in the figure of Jesus, who is about as divinely down-to-earth as you can get (though what he gained in approachability, he lost in grandeur).

On the other hand, in some ways Jesus was *more* exigent than his Father (turn the other cheek, sell-everything-and-give-it-to-the-poor, etc.) Whereas the Jewish God had eventually (in Isaiah 56.4-6) warmed to those "whose testicles are crushed or whose penis is cut off" (Deuteronomy 23.1, RSV) Jesus appeared to positively prefer "eunuchs which have made themselves' eunuchs for the klingdom of heaven's sake" (Matthew 19.12); and the Catholic Church took this hint and patented it, eventually lumping all sexually active non-eunuchs into a helot class known as the laity. (Meanwhile, it never occurred to God to inform his prophets, from Moses to Muhammad, that castrating young boys was a cruel and evil practice. The popes enjoyed the voices of the castrati in the Sixtine Chapel choir. Castration of slaves flourished all over the Islamic world, most notably perhaps in the Ottoman Empire, and as late as the 20th century the custodians of the tomb of the Prophet in Medina were black eunuchs. See Bernard Lewis, *Race and Slavery in the Middle East*, 1990). But Catholics led (and lead) the way when it came (and comes) to poisonous view of sexuality.

As if to compensate for such harshness, the Roman Church rendered God kinder and gentler by associating him with his wistful Virgin Mother, for whom Jesus (i.e., God) would always be, in the most flesh-and-blood sense, *her baby*. Finally, Muslims affirmed the process of internationalizing God (despite his dogged attachment to things Arabian and Arabic); and they made "merciful" and "compassionate" God's middle name (although in his signature disclosures to Muhammad, Allah often sounds rather gruff: see Chapter Sixteen, "The Death of Allah: A Consummation Devoutly to be Wished").

God eventually stopped saying anything for the record, though exactly when that happened is a matter of dispute. The Latter Day Saints will present a free copy of the Book of Mormon (penned many centuries after the closing of the Jewish, Christian, and Muslim canons) to anyone who asks, discreetly labeling it "Another Revelation of Jesus Christ." But if the Angel Moroni did contact Joseph Smith on God's behalf, the text strongly suggests that by 1830 God had lost his touch. In fact, any fair-minded critic graphing the quality of God's communiqués down through the ages would have to note a steady falling-off from the Old Testament to the New Testament to the Qur'an—and the less said about

Smith's laughable pastiche (where the resonant filler, "And it came to pass," occurs over 2,200 times), the better.

Apart from the canonical Scriptures, there have been a number of variations on the deity's image: The Gnostics' God shed as many (yecch) physical features as possible. The Crusaders' God (also popular with Cromwellians and Victorian imperialists) evoked the rousing exploits of Lord of Hosts. The Hassidic God loved to see bearded men—though not women—singing, drinking, and dancing; the Calvinist God abhorred it. The Lutheran God demanded total subordination to the state, as did the Catholic God—provided the ruler was himself Catholic. Puritans knew God was smiling on their political rebellions. Left-wing Latin-American Christians combined Marx and Jesus to get liberation theology, And as godless, dissolute modernity began to cast its baleful spell on the world, wave upon wave of fundamentalist reformers arose in every province of the Lord's earthly kingdom to call believers back to robotic conformity: Wahhabis, Catholic infallibilists, Southern Baptists, Haredim, etc. Their versions of The Most High, for all the sectarian differences, suggested some agreement: God is a peremptory stiff, an intolerant stickler, and really rather stupid—just like the fools who fabricated him.

Even the more humane and appealing versions of His majesty, especially the unfinished, evolving, doing-the-best-he-can God of some liberal believers and process theologians, are guilty—like all the others—of mirroring the various God-talkers themselves in their portraits and impersonations of The Divine. What else were believers supposed to do? Come to their senses and admit the absurdity of it all? Confess that they'd been fooling themselves all along? How often does *that* happen?

The obvious, inevitable objection arises to crush the whole garish pantheon of deities of every land and clime: If God were a reality like other, normal realities, like the nucleus of a cell, like the solar system, DNA, the circulation of the blood or capillary attraction; if God were like anything in nature, there would never be such wildly conflicting descriptions and accounts of "him." (That recurrent masculine pronoun is another giveaway.) Even if we assume that he has his inscrutable reasons for not clearing up the desperate, sometimes deadly confusion that prevails about his true character—for not holding a brief news conference to settle age-old theological divisions once and for all—even without some sort of helpful fatherly boost, you'd think that after so many contentious centuries, a clear picture of God would finally emerge.

But, of course, it hasn't—because there's no Divine Objective Correlative out there to measure all the versions of God against. It's a bit like the different images one sees of Sasquatch or the Abominable Snowman—though those imaginary creatures at least have bodies and habitats, which provides a minimal coherence to "reports" about them, unlike the disembodied, unlocatable, omniscient-but-aphasic, benign-but-irascible, divinely-wise-but-humanly-foolish First Cause that prophets shout about and theologians keep vainly trying to pin down. Alas (hurrah?), the real God will never stand up—because, like the nameless woman decried in the 1964 hit by the British pop-rock group, the Zombies, he's not there.

Chapter Four

God-Talk: The Wonderful World of Make-Believe

> But the most sagacious of the Christian theologians, the great Athanasius himself, has candidly confessed that, whenever he forced his understanding to meditate on the divinity of the *Logos*, his toilsome and unavailing efforts recoiled on themselves; that the more he thought, the less he comprehended; and the more he wrote, the less capable was he of expressing his thoughts. In every step of the inquiry we are compelled to feel and acknowledge the immeasurable disproportion between the size of the object and the capacity of the human mind. We may strive to abstract the notions of time, of space, and of matter, which so closely adhere to all the perceptions of our experimental knowledge. But as soon as we presume to reason of infinite substance, of spiritual generation, as often as we deduce any positive conclusions from a negative idea, we are involved in darkness, perplexity, and inevitable contradiction .
>
> —Gibbon, *Decline and Fall of the Roman Empire*, Chapter xxi

> Orthodoxy is my doxy; heterodoxy is another man's doxy.
>
> —Bishop William Warburton (1698-1779)

It's hard to put this politely, so let's not: all God-talk (theo-logy) is nonsense. One can utter grammatically correct sentences about God; but they don't refer to anything in the outside world. For starters, the majority of statements about God are apophatic, i.e., they say what he is *not* : mortal, temporal, corporeal, imperfect or limited in any way. This isn't too helpful, since it just points toward outer space, (maybe to the Abell galaxy, aka 18351R 916, currently the remotest one known) and says, "Imagine what it might be like yonder—but you'll never get within ten billion light years of it." So there's the universe we know, and there's The Beyond, which transcends knowledge and experience. The logic is obvious: if God were graspable with our flimsy little empirical models and categories, how great could he be? Tacitus had a phrase for this: *omne ignotum pro magnifico,* whatever's unknown is taken to be magnificent—after all, there's no way to prove it isn't, so long as it remains unknown. So the chorus goes on, "All hail, O Eternal, Everlasting, Omnipotent, Omniscient, Omnipresent, Omnicompetent, Immutable, Impeccable, Invisible, Invincible, et cetera One!" Even the great grandad of western theology, St. Augustine, said: "It's a rare soul that, whatever it may say about [the Trinity] knows what it is talking about" (*Confessions* XIII, 11). Not so much rare as non-existent.

But the God-talkers can't maintain a modest silence (or they'd be out of a job), so they don't. And Christians are by far the most philosophically garrulous of the monotheists. (Judaism is more about doing mitzvot than doctrine; and it's been said that you can explain the basics of Islam to anyone in ten minutes.) This makes for long discursive creeds, 39 Articles-and-all-that, for funky dogmas about Incarnation (hypostatic union!) and Redemption (justification through faith!), the Trinity (circumincession!) and the sacraments (*ex opere operato*!), the clergy (seven Holy Orders!) and the laity (Church Militant! Church Triumphant!), Scripture (Protocanonical! Deuterocanonical!) and Tradition (*quod semper! quod ubique! quod ab omnibus!*)—territory best left to professionals. Here too, however, as with the purely negative theology explaining what God isn't, we have a profusion of holy hot air: We're told about Divine Persons making unfathomable decisions in the Bosom of Eternity with (naturally) no witnesses. We learn of miraculous "Dispensations," sublime, incomprehensible decrees issued for our welfare but without our knowledge by a Mysterious Providence. Here's a sample from the aforementioned Thirty-Nine Articles (finally thrashed out and vouchsafed to a grateful world in 1571):

XVII. Of Predestination and Election.
Predestination to Life is the everlasting purpose of God, whereby (before the foundations of the world were laid) he hath constantly decreed by his counsel secret to us, to deliver from curse and damnation those whom he hath chosen in Christ out of mankind, and to bring them by Christ to everlasting salvation, as vessels made to honour. Wherefore, they which be endued with so excellent a benefit of God, be called according to God's purpose by his Spirit working in due season: they through Grace obey the calling: they be justified freely: they be made sons of God by adoption: they be made like the image of his only-begotten Son Jesus Christ: they walk religiously in good works, and at length, by God's mercy, they attain to everlasting felicity.

As the godly consideration of Predestination, and our Election in Christ, is full of sweet, pleasant, and unspeakable comfort to godly persons, and such as feel in themselves the working of the Spirit of Christ, mortifying the works of the flesh, and their earthly members, and drawing up their mind to high and heavenly things, as well because it doth greatly establish and confirm their faith of eternal Salvation to be enjoyed through Christ as because it doth fervently kindle their love towards God: So, for curious and carnal persons, lacking the Spirit of Christ, to have continually before their eyes the sentence of God's Predestination, is a most dangerous downfall, whereby the Devil doth thrust them either into desperation, or into wretchedness of most unclean living, no less perilous than desperation.

Furthermore, we must receive God's promises in such wise, as they be generally set forth to us in Holy Scripture: and, in our doings, that Will of God is to be followed, which we have expressly declared unto us in the Word of God.

Whew. Clearly, once you pick up the lingo, you can chatter like this forever. Just assume that God, whom no one has seen or heard or felt or tasted or smelled, is all-powerful. (Isn't he?) Well, then he must have a BIG say—make that more or less the entire say—in our eternal destiny, right? So, he does (the all-absorbing issue of "preforeordestination," as Huck Finn called it); only now we have to try and figure what, if any, difference our own wriggling, writhing attempts to be or do good might make, since this was all set in stone "before the foundations of the earth were laid." (To which the canonical answer seems to be St. Augustine's, referring to the two "malefactors" crucified alongside Jesus: One thief was saved, do not despair; one thief was damned, do not presume.) It's at least a nice touch that the Anglican Church warns believers—the "curious and carnal," morally underachieving ones, anyway—not to fall into despair, which isn't just a pitiful mental state, but a mortal sin, because the despairer has the nerve to deny God's saving power. Meanwhile, though godly thoughts about Predestination and Election no doubt *are* "full of sweet, pleasant, and unspeakable comfort" for the saved, the Anglicans tiptoe around the scary old Catholic-Calvinistic themes of the topography and terrors of eternal damnation. All things considered, if you *had* to be a Christian, wouldn't the C. of E. be the way to go? Turn on the TV Sunday morning and consider the stomach-turning, low-low church alternatives on cable.

The fact that nobody can agree about dogma for long—even Judaism and Islam have sects, some rather bitterly, if not murderously, unhappy with the others—suggests that it has no basis in fact. When the disputes are irrational, there's no rational way to decide them. For example, what's in the canon and what's not (on what discursive basis can mere humans determine what God said or didn't say)? And what does the heaven-sent writing in the canon *mean*? How did Mary remain a virgin (*ante partum! in partu! post partum!*), with her scripturally attested minimum of six children (Matthew 13.55-56) after the birth of Jesus? What precisely were Moses' or Jesus' or Muhammad's *intentions* in their various inspired, apodictic declarations (if they ever made them)? And then what to think of that mile-long parade of false prophets (already a worry back in Deuteronomy 13), grand heresiarchs, and run-of-the-mill heretics, pseudo-messiahs, apostates, schismatics, teachers of error, and other objects of revulsion to the orthodox, that snakes its way through history?

Get your scorecard here! Korah & Co., Sadducees, Essenes, Ebionites, Karaites, Gnostics, Arians, Patripassians, Sabellians, Montanists, Monophysites, Marcionists, Docetists, Donatists, Adoptionists, Shiites, Druze, Isma'ilis, Yazidis, Cathars, Bogomils, Molinists, Shabbateans, Socinians, Quakers, Shakers, Unitarians, Mormons, Ahmadiyya, Baha'is, and on and on, till the last syllable of eristical-religious time. Many of the heterodox have paid for their deviant theology with their lives or blood (Priscillian of Ávila, a gnostic Manichaean-style ascetic, executed in 385, believed to be the first Christian killed for having dangerous ideas), though some have given as good as they got (the Arian Visigoths in Spain, say). And the inevitable question: why doesn't this sort of thing happen in biochemistry or electrical engineering? (Because scientists and technologists don't waste their time studying daydreams or hallucinations. Theism is built on nothing but hearsay, which is why it never stands up in the court of reason.)

At the crudest and liveliest level of theology you get the lush jungles of metaphor and myth where most believers live: the unashamedly anthropomorphic realm of Playdough-shaping creators, talking snakes, punitive Floods, gay-incinerating fire-and-brimstone storms from heaven, Good Shepherds, angelic courts and choirs bowing to the King of Kings, nighttime horseback rides to the Throne of God, stoning the Devil, houris disporting with the faithful in the five-star garden of Paradise, and the pièce de résistance, blockbuster Doomsdays. On the one hand, since all God-talk is perforce drenched with the speakers' humanity, why not just embrace the inevitable and wallow in merry anthropomorphism? Chop off that foreskin for the LORD, get washed and sloshed in the Blood of the Lamb, march around that God-haunted rock in Mecca. Yee-HAH!

On the other hand, how can anyone take such childishness seriously? By associating with people who themselves take it for granted, the sort of people who can't imagine that death might be the end of everything. Listen to any hocus-pocus long enough, and you may well find it growing on you. Then dress it up in the pseudo-rational raiment of theology; and you're in business. If you've got the gift of gab, you can write entire libraries of "systematic" God-talk. It wasn't till some point in the 19th century that the majority of books published were on any subject *except* religion. If you build it, they will come!

Such accumulated folly—the oracles and articles of faith disseminated and defended by generations of lunatics and their devotees—is bad enough in itself. But then the iron laws of present-day democratic politeness and political correctness swing into action; and the dicta of the theophiles are placed in a crystalline sphere, as Alexander Pope said, above the reach of sacrilegious hands. The high priests of multiculturalism (almost all of them unbelievers) have laid down the law: Everything venerated by "communities of faith"—especially Third World, postcolonial people of color—must be treated with tight-lipped awe, regardless of how much it flies in the face of that old bugaboo, logocentric secular common sense. Thus, in the Academy at least, one can criticize Southern Baptists, but be careful about the Salafists. Things *you* wouldn't be caught dead doing, like wearing a niqab or sacrificing a sheep or leaving food on a grave, are ipso facto precious traditions when done by members of a "protected class."

But, above all, one mustn't criticize God: That would be too crude, insensitive, gauche, retro, naïve.

Haven't you heard about Stephen Jay Gould's "non-overlapping magisteria"? Religion tells us how to go to heaven; science tells us how the heavens go, etc. Look at Pascal, Kierkegaard, Dostoyevsky, Bonhoeffer, Hans Küng, the Templeton Prize, the AAR. Pat Robertson's (and George Bush's) God may be beyond the pale, but what about Bishop Tutu's (and Barack Obama's)? If you can't muster any personal theistic belief (technically optional, except for those bent on election to public office in the USA), then you should at least display a congenial, irenic, non-threatening agnosticism.

This will never do. The age-old nakedness of the emperors of God-talk needs to be exposed. Hard-core Pledgers of Allegiance (Mr. Jefferson, tear down that wall between church and state!), Evangelical generals (no atheists at West Point!), right-wing TV hosts (Glenn Beck has seen the light!), professional Southerners ("Ah jess luv mah Lord!"), brainless bumper stickers ("God Bless America!") continue to sing out their excruciating harmonies; so it's time for some serious booing (Bill Maher and Penn Jillette , among others, are doing their part; George Carlin, alas, is no longer available.) Bloggers ride herd on the mainstream media. Non-partisan fact-checkers vet the ads in political campaigns for distortions and lies. *Consumer Reports* tests products so purchasers needn't be at the mercy of advertisers. The Government Accountability Office (sometimes) cuts through the fog of Washington's finances and exposes legislators' shenanigans. So why can't more critics challenge and expose the preposterous assertions of the God-talkers? Of course, that's not easy in a nation where more than half the people believe they have a personal guardian angel hovering over them 24/7 (http://abcnews.go.com/US/Story?id=5833399&page=1), like the sylphs in *The Rape of the Lock* or Jiminy Cricket in *Pinocchio*. Still, *somebody*'s got to call the bluff of the reckless theo-ranters. Enough make-believe already.

Chapter Five

Beating a Dead God

> *New struggles.*—For centuries after the Buddha died, his shadow was still pointed out in a cave—a huge, terrifying shadow. God is dead; but men being what they are, there may yet be caves where for millennia his shadow will be pointed out. And we, we still have to overcome his shadow too.
>
> —Nietzsche, *The Gay Science*, 108

Antitheism is a word that, like its not-so-distant relative, mortalism (which offends spell-checks everywhere), ought to be better known. "Atheists," strictly speaking, should be used to denote those blasé characters whom Nietzsche's madman encounters in the marketplace. Denying the existence of God for them is a ho-hum process, like ignoring Ptolemaic epicycles or Cartesian vortices—disdaining a harmless long-exploded crotchet. But since God is more than a mere category error or logical lapse, this won't do. God is an active fantasy in the minds of many powerful persons and groups; and, as such, he makes real things—some of them demonstrably bad things—happen in the real world. So, acknowledging his death and wishing to spread the news of that epochal event can't be reduced to a philosophical shrug.

God must, in fact, be actively combated—dead as he is. His imagined diktats against homosexuality, women's rights, pleasures and freedoms of all sorts, and any and all deific "competitors," if not quite as harmful as ever, are still causing a lot of trouble. No one needs to be reminded how many theomaniacs have lately taken to blowing themselves up, along with as many bystanders as possible. (Muslim suicide-bombers had a sort of Christian template in the 4th century Circumcellions, fanatical North African peasant revolutionaries who sought martyrdom at any cost., e.g., by attacking Roman soldiers while armed only with clubs.) And membership in the various branches of the Taliban, Muslim, Christian, Jewish, and Hindu, is way too high. The leaders, and often the rank and file too, of the parties of God (Hezbollah) and armies of the pure (Lashkar-e-Tayba) ventriloquize unceasingly: God says this, God says that. We know him, we hear him, just listen to him (us) thunder!

There's probably no way to cure such auto-intoxication: frontal assaults won't do, nor will abstract analyses. Perhaps a steady spray of pointed ridicule, though it won't immediately break the spell, can create a unwelcoming atmosphere in which the grosser kinds of theomania will sooner or later wither away (see Chapter Eighteen, "A Humorless God"). The obvious skeptical reminders have to be sent to sloppy-minded believers: How suspicious, for example, that with very rare exceptions, God speaks only to men; and that when he does, he tells them that *their* tribe or nation has been supremely, if not uniquely, favored. Why doesn't the LORD send teams of Balaams far and wide to make all peoples sit at the feet of his one true Elect? (And while he does take Balaam's ass into his counsels, God mostly ignores or disdains his best-behaved creatures, the non-human beasts—see Chapter Fourteen, "God Abuses Animals").

How handy that God inhabits the inaccessible, impregnable bastion of faith, above and beyond the vain assaults of reason. The heart, especially the Yahweh-, Jesus-, or Allah-loving heart, has its reasons, which reason cannot know. Organ music, please. Light those candles, lower those shades, close those eyes. "We can only glean," John Henry Newman admits in *The Grammar of Assent* (1870), "from the surface of the world some faint and fragmentary views [of God]." So, rather than come to the stark logical conclusion that "there is no Creator," let's plunge into the murky fideistic marshland of "conscience," where the Old Fellow is bound to be hiding. When we can't figure things out on our own, God simply has to reveal them to us—or, more likely, to his inner circle of enraptured votaries.

And how convenient that God's revelations coincide so beautifully with his prophets' needs and desires, for example, Allah's peculiar dispensation allowing Muhammad to marry his adopted son Zaid's luscious wife Zaynab (and ten or more other women, beyond the usual limit of four), or the polygynous dispensations handed down to Joseph Smith, David Koresh, Warren Jeffs, and their numerous ilk, in stark contrast to the implacable divine hatred of polyandry. Where would monotheistic womanizers be without the Lord?

How odd that in his many verbatim statements recorded by the prophets God's voice varies so wildly in tone, from hectoring (Amos) to bloodthirsty (Nahum) to psychedelic (Ezekiel) to drop-dead majestic (Isaiah II) to righteously rancorous (the Book of Revelation and much of the Qur'an). And, although being interesting isn't ever listed as one of the divine attributes, it's odd that the Almighty and All-Wise One should so often repeat himself: I Have Rules And Don't You Forget It! Better Watch Out! Repent Or Else! Don't Say I Didn't Warn You! You People Are SO Ungrateful! I Can Make Life REALLY Nice For My Friends And REALLY Nasty For My Enemies! Am I Great—Or What?! One more round of slavish applause! And so on, ad nauseam.

How curious that the Master of the Moral Order (see Chapter Six, "Don't Do as God Says—Or as He Does") forgot to tell all his emissaries that slavery is wrong, that the death penalty is despicable, that homophobia is sick, that women shouldn't be oppressed or animals mistreated. In the so-called Priestly sections of the Bible God (e.g., Exodus 35-40, Yahweh rattles on in stupefying detail about the adoration-equipment he requires, the interior decoration of his tabernacle, the technicalities of ritual purity, etc.; but he says not a word to Moses and the patriarchs about the education of girls. Why, it's almost as if his vision were as thoroughly befogged as theirs with the tribal bias of bygone days.

How neat (all the easier to understand him) that God so closely resembles an earthly (male) monarch: eager for flattery and outraged by resistance. Billions of believers bowing and scraping, gyrating and prostrating, lowering their heads and bending their knees, bending toward Mecca (Allah's corporate headquarters, see Chapter Sixteen, "The Death of Allah—A Consummation Devoutly to be Wished"), singing psalms and shouting hosannahs, *ad majorem Dei gloriam* (he just can't get enough), Hallelujah, Praise ye the Lord, Alhammdulillah, *Gott sei Dank*. etc. It's all worthy of Anna's sarcastic recitative in *The King and I:*

> Yes, Your Majesty;
> No, Your Majesty.
> Tell us how low to go, Your Majesty;
> Make some more decrees, Your Majesty,
> Don't let us up off our knees, Your Majesty.
> Give us a kick, if you please Your Majesty
> Give us a kick, if you would, Your Majesty
> Oh, That was good, Your Majesty!

In the Bible God takes a rather sour view of human kingship: he has Samuel, the last of the judges, warn the Israelites (1 Sam. 10.19) that opting for King Saul equals rejecting their only true king, himself. (Never mind that, as the ultimate absentee ruler, Yahweh makes a useless head of state). And indeed, according to the curmudgeonly chroniclers of 1 and 2 Kings, the monarchs of both the northern kingdom of Israel and the southern kingdom of Judah were almost all losers: active promoters—or inactive suppressors—of *the* most horrible sin, idolatry. But, wretched as the earthly model proved, Yahweh never lost his appetite for the fulsome praise accorded kings; and so the Book of Psalms resounds with it. "The LORD is King for ever and ever: the heathen are perished out of his land," etc. (Ps. 10.16), etc.

How fortunate, in a word, that believers have been so sweetly accepting of all the metaphors used to describe God, despite their utter inadequacy. God is a king (never a queen), even though real kings are arbitrarily chosen, autocratically obnoxious, and absurdly obsolete. God is a judge and legislator (bearded, never breasted) even though real judges don't make laws, and real legislators are forever revoking and amending their predecessors' statutes. God is a father (never a mother), even though with time real fathers surrender their authority and let their sons run the show. God is a shepherd (never a milkmaid), even though real shepherds dine on lamb. God is a warrior (never an amazon), even though real warriors can never do good except by doing harm. And so on.

This isn't just quibbling. Apologists for God will often spin a variation on Flaubert's image of speech as beating out tunes on cracked kettles to make bears dance when we really want to move the stars to tears—i.e., the fault lies in the desperately inadequate medium of language—but that won't do. There's no reason to believe in some splendid divine realm hinted at in the maunderings of the devout. God is no more and no less than what the people who claim to have contacted him say he is. You'd think that four thousand years or so would be long enough for them to draw a coherent Identikit likeness of the deity. Well, those many contacts have in fact sketched a picture—but it's neither coherent nor pretty.

Whence the job of antitheism: to analyze and then shred that "image and likeness" in which we've supposedly been created; and which turns out—surprise, surprise—to be no more than a series of reflections in a mirror, but raised to a ludicrous and toxic power. The Torah frowns in vain on representing God by "any graven image, or any likeness of anything that is in heaven above, or that is in the earth beneath, or that is in the water under the earth" (Exodus 20.4). Islam goes one step further and bans images of Muhammad (though if he lived in the West today he'd soon find his face in a police booking photo, what with his nine-year-old child bride Aisha). But it's too late: There's no way for humans to do without images—for better or worse, it's how they think. Both the Bible and the Qur'an are full of direct or implied images of God; and, as mentioned, they're ugly, not to say hateful: a high-testosterone psychopath, drunk on delusions of grandeur, obstreperous, violent, preachy, cliquish, irresponsible. You get the idea—antitheists, fire when ready. Lord knows he deserves it: he's got a rap sheet as long as the history of the world.

Chapter Six

Don't Do as God Says—or as He Does

> If any man take a wife, and go in unto her, and hate her, And give occasions of speech against her, and bring up an evil name upon her, and say, I took this woman, and when I came to her, I found her not a maid: Then shall the father of the damsel, and her mother, take and bring forth the tokens of the damsel's virginity unto the elders of the city in the gate: And the damsel's father shall say unto the elders, I gave my daughter unto this man to wife, and he hateth her; And, lo, he hath given occasions of speech against her, saying, I found not thy daughter a maid; and yet these are the tokens of my daughter's virginity. And they shall spread the cloth before the elders of the city. And the elders of that city shall take that man and chastise him; And they shall amerce him in an hundred shekels of silver, and give them unto the father of the damsel, because he hath brought up an evil name upon a virgin of Israel: and she shall be his wife; he may not put her away all his days. But if this thing be true, and the tokens of virginity be not found for the damsel: Then they shall bring out the damsel to the door of her father's house, and the men of her city shall stone her with stones that she die: because she hath wrought folly in Israel, to play the whore in her father's house: so shalt thou put evil away from among you.
>
> —Deuteronomy 22.13-21

> Those that make war against God and His apostle and spread disorder in the land shall be slain or crucified or have their hands and feet cut off on alternate sides, or be banished from the land.
>
> —Qur'an 5:33

In the minds of most believers God is all about being and doing good. Consummately good himself, he tells us, as always through his inspired emissaries, what's right and what's wrong, and what happens when we obey or disobey his rules. But all this opens a gigantic can of worms.

First of all, *is* God good? His sacred texts certainly show him inflicting a massive amount of damage and pain on his beloved (?) creatures, both in this world (the Flood, plagues, military disasters, exile, etc.) and the next (eternal hell). Watching the nightly news points up what look like terrible engineering flaws in the grand design of creation (senseless violence, natural catastrophes, AIDS, etc.) But, even assuming that this is due to our creaturely misperception, God-as-the-foundation-of-the-moral-order is a hoary old notion that has long since gone down for the count.

Plato delivered the most damaging body-blow to it in the *Euthyphro*, where Socrates poses an inescapable dichotomy: Either the gods approve what's right just because it *is* right, in which case their (his) relation to the moral order roughly parallels that of a *Good Housekeeping* seal on a consumer product or an Underwriters Lab sticker on an appliance. Neither *makes* the object safe or effective; they just bear witness to the prior fact that it *is* safe or effective. So God's approval of moral laws would be no more than a powerful endorsement—nice to have, but in no way essential. One might even say that, like any honest person called into court to testify, God had no choice but to acknowledge the truth as he found it. Anything less would be perjury.

On the other hand, if the gods' (God's) approbation of any behavior was what *made* it moral, then morality would be arbitrary: God would just so happen to like or dislike certain things, thereby rendering them good or bad. Ethics would then be something like a list of God's personal preferences, the equivalent of a sweet tooth or a yen for kinky sex. No believer would ever accept *that* sort of absurd relativism (inter alia, it would mean that the majority of earthlings without access to the Bible could never figure out what the right thing was). So God might be a cheerleader for morality, but not its inventor.

Still, that's just the beginning of it. The eternal, perfect laws revealed by God to Moses (later endorsed in toto by Jesus in Mt. 5.18: "For verily I say unto you, till heaven and earth pass, one jot or one tittle shall in no wise pass from the law ") and Muhammad have a depressingly predictable way of looking their age: They're flat-out sexist (total subjection of women to men, polygyny, "purification" rites after childbirth, mandatory silence in worship, etc.) They call for all sorts of cruel and pointless bloody sacrifices of birds and animals. (see Chapter Fourteen, "God Abuses Animals").They strongly favor capital punishment. They insist on non-stop flattery of, and self-abasement before, the LORD. They divide the world up into the favored Us (Israelites, Christians, Muslims) and the despised Them (gentiles, pagans, kaffirs). They almost completely ignore the non-human world, except as lens for admiring the Creator. And they validate their claims by appealing to nonsensical mythic "history" (daily [except Shabbes] delivery of manna for forty years, Jesus' resurrection from the dead, Muhammad's guileless retelling of the the Seven Sleepers of Ephesus fairy tale in surah 18).

And what is one to make of God's complete failure to inform his interlocutors that slavery was a bad idea? In the very next chapter of Exodus (21) after the Ten Commandments, Yahweh lays out the rules for slave-holding ("When you buy a male Hebrew slave . . ."). St. Paul sent the runaway slave Onesimus back to his owner Philemon with a little note. Muhammad saw no need to abolish slavery; and over the next thirteen centuries Muslim traders collected more African slaves than the Christian traders did, though they generally treated them better.

The obvious conclusion is that at bottom God has nothing to do with morality. "Inspired" (i.e., fanatical) males use God as a p.a. system to proclaim their own and their culture's beliefs about behavior. "Law," it appears, doesn't have enough majesty all by itself; it has to be enhanced with all sorts of special effects, as in the awesome, go-for-broke scene from Exodus 19.16, 18-19: ". . . there were thunders and lightning, and a thick cloud upon the mount, and the voice of the trumpet exceedingly loud, so that all the people that was in the camp trembled. . . . And mount Sinai was altogether on a smoke, because the LORD descended upon it in fire: and the smoke thereof ascended as the smoke of a furnace, and the whole mount quaked greatly. And when the voice of the trumpet sounded long, and waxed louder and louder, Moses spoke and God answered him by voice." Kowabunga.

Alas, there's no empirical evidence that once the sound-and-light show ended, believing made the Israelites better persons (right after Yahweh's theophany they took to dancing around the golden calf—and God knows what else—although for non-believers it's hard to see what's so horrific about idolatry). By contrast, we have tons of evidence that passionate religious belief can fuel moral blindness, mass murder and persecution (see Chapter Nine, "Holy Wars: God's Olympics").

In reply, apologists for religion will argue that past or present outrages committed by theomaniacs don't reflect the "true spirit" of Judaism, Christianity, or Islam. The "real" versions of theism are responsible only for first-rate deportment, such as kindness to strangers, charitable donations, self-restraint, and peace-making, things that everyone can, no, must, approve of (because the only reliable, long-term gauge of moral value is concrete results). But if results are what matter, then no one needs God to understand or appreciate ethics. In other words, the best criterion for religious morality is secular reason.

Then there's the old question, Does belief in a God who sends the righteous to heaven and the wicked to hell have any actual effect on behavior? There are doubtless too many variables and imponderables here to settle the issue "scientifically." But, since the death penalty, which is a lot more immediate than the most vivid sermons on hell, fails to deter murderers, why should the mere imagined prospect of post-mortem karma alter anyone's behavior, especially when most moral agents don't plan on dying any time soon? (Besides, there's no dodging a guilty verdict in an earthly court; whereas God can always wipe away the supernatural guilt and punishment payable for even the worst of felonies. Whence the epitaph of that lucky 17th century English Christian gunned down in the Civil Wars but blessed by an instant "act of contrition": "Betwixt the stirrup and the ground,/ Mercy I asked, mercy I found." O beatific buzzer-beater!)

Then too, the foundation of theistic morality, the Torah, derives from a time when there was no belief in the survival of the individual after death. After they expire, all the patriarchs in the Bible simply get "gathered to their people"—end of story. The pay-off for good behavior had to come in the here and now, but the Bible itself (Job 21.7-15, Jeremiah 12.1-4, Ecclesiastes 4.1) admits that this doesn't necessarily happen. Virtue, it seems, must be its own reward—like it or not, take it or leave it.

But, despite any theoretical otherworldly rewards and punishments, human beings by and large do what their genes, culture, and circumstances make them do. *What* they do can be evaluated in many ways, but the most sensible one seems to be the approach taken by consequentialism, laconically defined by Peter Singer in *Practical Ethics* (1993) as the principle that, "I must choose the course of action that has the best consequences, on balance, for all affected." This formula, needless to say, is only the beginning. The utilitarian endeavor to "maximize the interests" of everyone involved (which has to include animals) calls for adding up costs and benefits, for comparison-contrast, study and debate, trial and error; and it won't ever win universal consensus or prevent all or even most mistakes. In the overwhelming majority of cases we act (and have to act) by rules of thumb, or what Singer calls playing "percentage tennis": giving what on average seems likely to be one's best shot in each situation.

This is a messy arrangement (when were human affairs anything else?), but there's no rational alternative. We can't take orders from God, because he can't and doesn't give any. The ones he's on record as giving all come from his prophetic impersonators and are smeared with *their* fingerprints, for instance, his unspeakably obnoxious rule in Deuteronomy 22 about stoning brides who lack a hymen. Lest you think that dictate as passé as it's disgusting, the *New York Times* of June 11, 2008 reports that the going [discounted] rate for hymenoplasty in Paris, a procedure in great demand from anxious Muslim fiancées, is $2,900. The great tradition marches on.

Americans can't seem to shake the dumb, dogged belief that one way or another God *must* be connected to good behavior. Hence they warmly support posting the Ten Commandments in public, something like a celestially stamped "No Parking" sign. You know, what with our young people these days losing touch with the Old Values, every little bit helps. Alas, the Decalogophiles seem to forget how little good the Commandments did their original recipients: Of the entire generation of adults present at the foot of Mount Sinai/Horeb, all but two, Joshua and Caleb, were doomed to die before entering the Promised Land because they disrespected Yahweh. Of the twelve tribes that eventually made their way into Canaan, ten were scattered and lost forever in 722 BCE when the Northern Kingdom of Israel was destroyed by the Assyrians. The tribes of Judah and Benjamin were spared—but only to be subjected to horrible divine (or was it?) scourges, from the siege of Jerusalem in 586 BCE to the Jewish War of 66-70, the Bar Kochba revolt, the Crusades, the depredations of Bogdan Khmelnitsky, the Russian pogroms, the Holocaust . . . Much good the Ten Commandments did the Jews!

The most curious feature of this rhapsodic link between God and goodness is that it continues without a shred of evidence that the Great Divine Promoter of Morality is doing, or has ever done, a damn thing to help the cause along. Theomaniacs give God credit for things no one ever witnessed (creation, miracles), and for victories in war (like the slaughter of the Midianites by Gideon [Judges 7.19-23] or Muhammad's triumph over the Meccans in the battle of Badr [Qur'an 3:123]). They claim that he whispers divine thoughts into his servants' ears (as when he told Samuel to anoint Saul or Elijah to anoint Jehu—though he later decided that both were bad ideas). They tell cautionary tales of punishment being dished out to evildoers: Uzzah struck dead for touching the ark of the covenant (2 Samuel 6.6-7), and Herod Agrippa zapped by an angel (Acts 12.20-23) for not "giving God the glory." But when did God or Allah, in post-biblical or post-Qur'anic times, ever intervene to help the would-be virtuous, for instance, by providing funds so that hungry people wouldn't have to steal or prostitute themselves?

This is hardly a new objection, of course. The Bible itself raises it again and again—without ever coming up with an answer. Ecclesiastes writes: "So I returned and considered all the oppressions that are done under the sun: and behold the tears of such as were oppressed, and they had no comforter; and on the side of their oppressors there was power, but they had no comforter" (4.1). No comforter? But what about God the Merciful, the Compassionate? M.i.a., as usual. Yet theologians don't see a problem in the way their invisible, infinitely remote Sacred Spook threatens to land on sinners with the concentrated mass of Mount Everest for their transgressions, without ever having helped to keep them on the proverbially hazardous, incredibly demanding strait and narrow path.

How to explain such divine harshness, as nasty as it's incomprehensible? One of the classic arguments by the God-talkers is that evil (suffering, misery, agony, etc.) is just the necessary downside to free will (and who can doubt that we have *that*?) As Milton's odious God declares to the heavenly hosts in Book III of *Paradise Lost,* humans were created "Sufficient to have stood, though free to fall." Oh sure, God knows in advance that his hapless creatures are going to stumble into one catastrophe after another, but he insists on letting them flounder:

> Not free, what proof could they have giv'n sincere
>   Of true allegiance, constant faith or love,
>   Where only what they needs must do appeared,
>   Not what they would? What praise would they receive?
>   What pleasure I from such obedience paid,
>   When will and reason (reason also is choice),

Useless and vain, of freedom both despoiled,
Made passive both, had served necessity,
Not me.

(ll.99, 103-111)

Thus God the Egomaniac: he doesn't care whether mortals are happy (hell, he's certain they won't be); he just wants them to join the footlicking chorus around his imperial throne. However staggering the cost in blood, tears, and treasure, he's quite content to see us pay it. What an immoral monster—whence the need to get rid of him, permanently.

Chapter Seven

God is Spirit—But What's That?

> The Vatican Council has explained the meaning to be attributed to the term mystery in theology. It lays down that a mystery is a truth which we are not merely incapable of discovering apart from Divine Revelation, but which even when revealed, remains "hidden by the veil of faith and enveloped, so to speak by a kind of darkness" (Constitution, "De fide cath.," iv). In other words, our understanding of it remains only partial, even after we have accepted it as part of the Divine message. Through analogies and types we can form a representative concept expressive of what is revealed, but we cannot attain that fuller knowledge which supposes that the various elements of the concept are clearly grasped and their reciprocal compatibility manifest. As regards the vindication of a mystery, the office of natural reason is solely to show that it contains no intrinsic impossibility, that any objection urged against it on the score that it the laws of thought is invalid. More than this it cannot do.
>
> The Vatican Council further defined that the Christian faith contains mysteries strictly so called (can. 4). All theologians admit that the doctrine of the Trinity is of the number of these.
>
> —Article on "The Blessed Trinity" (G. Joyce),
> in *The Catholic Encyclopedia* (1912)

Throughout the far-flung, arcane kingdom of God-talk there isn't a stranger principality than Trinitarianism, where even the most plausible theo-babblers plunge into incoherence and lose themselves in unfathomable obscurity. *O altitudo!* "Explaining" Yahweh & Son is a fairly straightforward business (Creator-Redeemer, Heavenly Boss-Earthly Rep, Justice-Mercy, etc.), so long as we discount some of Jesus' Arian-sounding remarks (like Mark 10.18, "Why do you call me good? No one is good but God alone"). But adding on that Holy Spirit, the Divine Wind that bloweth where it listeth (John 3.8) as an actual, separate person seriously complicates things.

The good news is that pneumatology, whose most recondite abysses we can, like most believers, ignore, brings us to the very heart of theism; for as John 4.24 says. "God *is* spirit." And the most important thing to know about spirit is that it, strictly speaking, doesn't exist. "Spirit" is a fine example of what Alfred North Whitehead called "the fallacy of misplaced concreteness." Most words for "spirit"—*ruach, pneuma, spiritus, esprit* (and other Romance-language forms), *dusha, Geist, ghost*, etc.—come from roots that mean wind or breath of air. So far, so good.

The fallacy here grows out of the pseudo-logical assumption that just as the wind, however invisible in itself, is undoubtedly real (look at those leaves swishing back and forth), so there must be some real-but-not-physical entity outside the observable universe that controls it, even as there must be some real-but-not-physical soulish principle inside our bodies that controls them.

It stands to reason, or it used to, before the rise of science. At first glance, all sorts of mental and intellectual phenomena, speech, thought, memory, dreams, creation and invention, etc. must appear godlike and inexplicable; and many people still see them that way. But as we learn more about the brain and neurology in general, we understand that there's no need to hypostatize synaptic firings into some mysterious, eternal SOUL (which starts in time, but lives on forever in heaven or hell). Computers and cats have memories, and so do we. Dogs dream as well as humans. Animals and insects communicate all the time, and so on and so forth. Ockham's razor slices that fuzzy, fluffy, immaterial butterfly (one of the meanings of the Greek word *psyche*) out of our heads for good. Once it's removed and discarded, you'll never miss it.

The Spirit goes whooshing through the entire Bible, from the time when it sits brooding over the face of the deep in Genesis till the great ecclesiastical *coup de théâtre* when it swoops down on the heads of Jesus' disciples in the reversed Tower-of-Babel episode known as Pentecost—and blasts or wafts its way clear through the Acts of the Apostles and Revelation. Prophets, judges (the holy warriors, not the jurists), and princes get filled with the Spirit, but practically no women. (Revelation

2.20 chides the bishop of Thyatira for allowing "that woman Jezebel, which calleth herself a prophetess, to seduce my servants to commit fornication, and to eat things sacrificed to idols.")

After being thus electrically zapped, the charismatic individual then chops or tears to pieces a yoke of oxen (Saul in 1 Sam 11.6-7), a lion (Samson in Judges 14.5-6), a thousand Philistines (Samson again in Judges 15.14-15), an Ammonite army (Jephthah in Judges 11.29-33), or whatever. The prophet Ezekiel seems to have flown "in the Spirit" around Jerusalem, as well as back and forth from Jerusalem to Babylon (ca. 400 miles); but that was a gentler flight than Habakkuk's, whom the angel of the Lord grabbed by the hair of his head and tugged through the sky from Judea to Babylon (to serve dinner to Daniel in the lions' den [Bel and the Dragon vv. 33-39, Daniel 14. 32-38 in the Vulgate]).

But far more often, a Spirit-struck individual simply gets "inspired," i.e., God breathes into his mouth, and out gushes a stream of godly words. Or at least that's how the ravers and ranters and religious poets of ancient Israel liked to describe it. In a semi-similar vein, pagan bards appealed to the Muses for inspiration (it's notable that the original Hebrew word for spirit *ruach* is feminine, like the Muses; and there is even a 14th century depiction of *die heilige Geistin*, the Holy Ghostess [from Unterschalling in Upper Bavaria], a cheerfully zaftik feminine member of the Blessed Trinity. As baby-makers, women inevitably symbolize the creative process.) John Milton went one step further by invoking Urania, the Heavenly Muse, who combined the functions of *ruach ha-kodesh* and the patroness of epic, Calliope, by drawing upon the wellsprings of both the Bible and classical literature, and who was in fact none other than Milton's own fertile brain. (Left to their own masculine devices, men can't create anything at all.)

The bottom line once more is that there *is* no spirit, not in the personified divine sense nor in the misty-mystical sense of intangible-stuff-that-transcends-matter. "Spirit" once worked as a nebulous description for any hard-to-understand thing, from lightning to thinking. As our powers of description improve (despite their deep interest in reproduction, the authors of the Bible and the Qur'an knew nothing of the ovum—among other things), we don't need to fall back on cartoonish folk explanations. Of course, science doesn't actually "explain" the world either, in any definitive or final way: It draws increasingly fuller and more helpful diagrams; so we don't have to waste our time on, say, the goofy theistic gynecology that has God "opening" and "closing" wombs at will

(Gen. 29.31, 1 Sam. 1.5), impregnating virgins, and other modes of showing off.

Not content with their fairy tales about miraculous divine interventions (all of which, even if true, could be dismissed as trivial, given their extreme rarity and antiquity), believers typically insist on badmouthing "matter" because of its supposed inferiority to spirit. The New Testament—and Christian tradition thereafter—likes to talk condescendingly about "the flesh" (often lumped together with "the world, " as in, "All that is in the world , the lust of the flesh and the lust of the eyes and the pride of life" [1 John 1.16] and the ever-popular, though non-existent, Devil), as if "the flesh" were some wretched Brand X, and spirit the deluxe, top-of-the-line make. Or maybe "the flesh" is an immature, repulsive phase, like adolescence, full of sulking, self-pity, and acne, ideally to be followed by serene "spiritual" adulthood.

Listening to theists pontificate about "mere matter" reminds one of ex-Senator Ted Stevens defining the Internet as "a series of tubes"—they're ignorant blowhards. Asked about DNA, brain chemistry, subatomic particles, or the Big Bang, they'll say either, "That's not my department," or "How wonderful God's works are!"—which completely misses, or dishonestly dodges, the point: The universe can get along very well without its mythical Mover and Shaker, but not vice versa. In the topsy-turvy cosmology of theism the billions of life forms laboriously developed over hundreds of millions years of evolution are chalked up to the "will" of the Divine Demiurge, while the dazzling complexity of everyday things like weather (except the weather on Mount Sinai), blood (except for Jesus' "most precious" blood), or wine ("abominations devised by Satan" Qur'an 5:90) is either despised or ignored.

How emancipating, then, to listen to Nietzsche sweep away the cobwebs of "spirituality" with his industrial-strength broom: "In Christianity neither morality nor religion make contact with reality at any point. One gets nothing but imaginary causes ('God,' 'soul,' 'the ego,' 'spirit,' 'free will'—or 'unfree will'); and all sorts of imaginary effects ('redemption,' 'grace,' 'punishment,' 'forgiveness of sin'). One gets intercourse between imaginary beings ("God,' 'spirits,' 'souls'), imaginary natural science (anthropocentric and completely lacking the concept of natural causes), imaginary psychology (all sorts of self-misunderstandings, interpretations of pleasant and unpleasant common feelings . . . , 'repentance,' 'remorse,' 'temptation by the Devil,' 'the presence of God'), and imaginary teleology ('the kingdom of God,' 'Judgment Day,' 'eternal life.') This purely fictional world differs—and greatly to its own disadvantage—from the world of dreams in that the latter mirrors reality, whereas the former falsifies, devalues, and denies it" (*The Antichrist*, 15).

My, doesn't *that* clear the air. Just throw all the old spirit-claptrap out the window (it's lighter than air, so it'll just float away); and you'll never miss it. It clarifies nothing that science doesn't clarify infinitely better. It tells you nothing you didn't know already, and it just fogs up your glasses when you're trying to get a good look at the world. The biblical cosmography of believers was always an elaborate doodle, never a road map.

Many of today's faithful, of course, while wavering in their faith, shrink from the thought of renouncing all the spirit-images forever (even as their godparents, speaking on their infant-behalf, renounced the pomps and works of Satan when they were baptized). It does seem rather a loss, you know, like all those funky-splendid religious canvases in the galleries of the Louvre or the Prado. Can't we just enjoy this stuff for its beauty?

But that's exactly the point: Religion belongs in a museum, not of art, but of anthropology (like the great one in Mexico City). Yes, there are countless millions of misguided people who take it all literally—but by the same token there are Orthodox Jews who want to rebuild the Temple of Jerusalem so as to continue the animal sacrifices (the perfect, unblemished red heifer to remove corpse pollution!) prescribed by the Law (Numbers 18.2-10!) and put on hold ever since 70 CE. There are Catholic fanatics in the Philippines who have themselves (temporarily) crucified as part of Passion Week; and thousands of deranged Shiites beat themselves bloody with whips on the feast of Ashurah in a masochistic reenactment of Husayn ibn Ali's "martyrdom" in 680. No museums for these folks!

Those are the sorts of sensations, along with various flashes or twinges of joy, grief, and excitement sparked by less violent devotion, that do indeed get lost when one gives up the delusions of faith for clear-eyed life in the sublunary world. But it's a fair exchange. To quote Freud, quoting Heine, in *The Future of an Illusion:* "As for heaven, we'll leave it/ To the angels and the sparrows." Like spirit (and "spirituality," insofar as the word means anything more than "ways of thinking") it's all hot air.

Chapter Eight

God Falling Short?
Extrapolate, Extrapolate!

> Wherefore do the wicked live, become old, yea, are mighty in power? Their seed is established in their sight with them, and their offspring before their eyes. Their houses are safe from fear, neither is the rod of God upon them. Their bull gendereth, and faileth not; their cow calveth, and casteth not her calf. They send forth their little ones like a flock, and their children dance. They take the timbrel and harp, and rejoice at the sound of the organ. They spend their days in wealth, and in a moment go down to the grave. Therefore they say unto God, Depart from us; for we desire not the knowledge of thy ways. What is the Almighty, that we should serve him? and what profit should we have, if we pray unto him?
>
> —Book of Job 21.7-15

Job's complaints were never answered by Yahweh—who just told him to shut his mouth, mind his own business, and admire the mysteries of Creation, many of which (like when the wild goats of the rock bring forth) have by now been figured out (late May to early June)—nor by any of his votaries. Even the cheeriest theomavens have to admit that it takes strong faith (i.e., wild suggestibility) to discern the presence and activity of God in the bloody spectacle of history, past and present. Women, for example, have always been more or less ground down at all times and in all places (and quite frequently in the name of God). Justice of any kind has always been hard to come by (the Bible and the Qur'an are comfortable with divinely sponsored bloodshed—see Chapter Nine, "Holy Wars:

God's Olympics"). There's always been a deadly disconnect between evolution and civilization, as nature bred into human males ineradicable habits of aggressiveness and selfishness that had survival value hundreds of thousands of years ago out on the African savannahs, but that don't work so well on a crowded planet bristling with WMDs. And then, as usual, there are the thousand natural shocks that flesh is heir to (mitigated in modern times by "quality medical care," psychopharmacology, and health insurance, along with the time-tested remedies of suicide and booze, but also intensified by various kinds of destructive machines—cars, guns, IEDs and so forth). Why does the Lord let so much poisonous shit happen?

The traditional method for getting God off this hook is by radical extrapolation. Take every cubic centimeter of beauty and goodness you find and multiply it to infinity: it's the ultimate in fuzzy math. Thus, St. Paul went way too far when he asserted in Romans 1.20 that, "Ever since the creation of the world his [God's] eternal power and divine nature, invisible though they are, have been understood and seen through the things he has made. So they [pagan unbelievers] are without excuse" (RSV).Really? And how do we know "he" made them? St. Thomas Aquinas in his Five Demonstrations was more honest when he said that nature does show us that God exists, but only "in a general and confused way."

That's probably the way most believers view the situation; and even America's favorite pantheistic infidel, Walt Whitman, nodded ironically in the direction of such thinking when he wrote in *Song of Myself* (6), in response to the child's question, "What is the grass?":

> I guess it is the handkerchief of the Lord,
> A scented gift and remembrancer designedly dropt,
> Bearing the owner's name someway in the corners, that we may see and remark and say, *Whose*?

But what about the snakes, fleas, ticks (not to mention toxic pesticides from Chemlawn) in that grass? Finding God, or traces of him, in nature has kept apologists busy for centuries; but all such arguments received a staggering karate-chop from David Hume's *Dialogues Concerning Natural Religion* (1779). There Hume's stand-in, Philo, points out that if we define God from the evidence found in nature, then we have to attribute *everything*, good, bad, or indifferent, to his doing; and we have no right to imagine him one whit better than his handiwork. As he deflates the naïve deist, Cleanthes, Philo says: "A man who follows your hypothesis is able, perhaps, to assert, or conjecture, that the universe sometimes arose from something like design. But beyond that position he cannot ascertain one single circumstance, and is left afterwards to fix every point of his theology by the utmost license of fancy and hypothesis. This world, for aught he knows, is very faulty and imperfect, compared to a superior standard; and was only the first rude essay of an infant Deity, who afterwards abandoned it, ashamed of his lame performance; it is the work only of some dependent, inferior Deity; and is the object of derision to his superiors; it is the production of old age and dotage in some superannuated Deity; and ever since his death, has run on at adventures, from the first impulse and active force, which it received from him . . ." (Part V).

Now there's a line for God's obituary: "An apprentice world-maker, he eventually lost interest in his rather primitive early work; and, stung by criticism from more architecturally skilled deities, he left planet earth and its surroundings to their own hapless devices." By this interpretation, humans and everything else might be something like the Baronci family of Florence that Boccaccio speaks of in the *Decameron* VI, 6): they were the most unsightly creatures on earth because they were God's first floundering attempts to draw—later on, when he made other folks, his rudimentary skills improved. Now if we Baroncinians could only come across a new and improved universe (inhabited perhaps by Nietzschean *Übermenschen*), we might feel better about our troubles. But alas, the much dreamed-of Intelligent Designer doesn't exist; and the odds of our finding a randomly evolved better cosmos look slim-to-none.

Another classic response to the slings and arrows of outrageous—or just garden-variety—fortune has been to blame the victim: argue back from the evidence of "sin" to a sufficient cause of our troubles. The *fons et origo* of such loopy thinking is the Christian myth of the Fall, or Genesis 3 as hijacked by Paul of Tarsus and Augustine of Hippo and then epically twisted and embellished by John Milton and a million priests, preachers, and apologists. As fans of *Forensic Files* and similar programs know, there's nothing more frustrating than an unsolved crime. So it comes as a sort of grim satisfaction to learn that, when push comes to shove, *we* are the perpetrators of the human condition. (Of course, up to a point we actually are—only not in the way the theologians think.) In Adam's fall we sinned all.

Heaven only knows—the God-talkers tell us—how splendid our prelapsarian life would have been had it not been for, well, you know, the naked little lady and her moment of typical female weakness in Eden. Blaise Pascal had to admit that the doctrine of original sin was, on the face of it, absurd; but there was, he thought, no other way to make sense of the unstoppable pyroclastic flow of human misbehavior. Oh really? How about testosterone, aided and abetted by high- or low-tech weaponry and all the idols of the Francis Bacon Quartet (Tribe, Cave, Marketplace, and Theater) in all their cacophonic frenzy? How about the short-sighted human brain, which even now continues to promote and preside over such brutal follies as the arms race, overpopulation, and the trashing of the planet? How about all the accumulated toxic -isms of history?

In the end, this last-ditch strategy doesn't work. You can't get there from here—we're stuck with what we have. When Cleanthes objects to Philo that, gosh, a lot of times we see fragmentary evidence, such as a footprint, from which we can fairly posit the full-grown, normal-limbed human body that must have left it (Friday's tracks on the beach in *Robinson Crusoe*); or we see a half-built house, and we know a builder must have spent some time on the premises. So, perhaps this world is God's footprint or incomplete edifice. No, says Philo, we can make that inference only because we've seen bodies and buildings before. So far as we know, there's only one universe, which can't be compared with, or measured against, anything else. So we have no justification for projecting our little human-sized fantasies onto everything outside us. We can't give God the benefit of the doubt (well, a million doubts) because he's not a known quantity (apart from his fictional life in Scripture and folklore).

So, we're back to where we began: the bramble bush, mud-puddle-weed patch of life as it is, sans glimmering utopian horizons to retrospectively justify the grief and horror, minus any magical spells to undo the havoc once and still being done. And farewell to making excuses for God. In his preface to *Major Barbara* (1907) Shaw attacked the prison system by contrasting the way we treat dogs who bite and humans who commit violent crimes. "We do not imprison dogs," he says in his Modest-Proposal way, "We even take our chance of their first bite. But if a dog delights to bark and bite, it goes to the lethal chamber. That seems to me sensible." No "correctional facility" for canines, to be tortured as we do humans. So, instead of imprisoning criminals, he says, "It would be far more sensible to put up with their vices, as we put up with their illnesses, until they give more trouble than they are worth, at which point we should, with many apologies and expressions of sympathy, and some generosity in complying with their last wishes, then, place them in the lethal chamber and get rid of them."

To which my rejoinder would be: and why not do the same to God? Having long since reached the point where he—or the idea of him—gives more trouble than he (it) is worth, the sanest thing would be to get rid of him, as many thoughtful people have already done. God-talkers might protest, but dyslexics would remind us that "dog" and "God" are interchangeable. Time to put him down.

Chapter Nine

Holy Wars: God's Olympics

> If you hear in one of your cities which the LORD your God gives you to dwell there, that certain base fellows have gone out among you and have drawn away the inhabitants of the city, saying, "Let us go and serve other gods," which you have not known, then you shall inquire and make search and ask diligently; and behold, if it be true and certain that such an abominable thing has been done among you, you shall surely put the inhabitants of that city to the sword, destroying it utterly, all who are in it and all its cattle, with the edge of the sword. You shall gather all its spoil into the midst of its open square, and burn the city and all its spoil with fire, as a while burnt offering to the LORD your God; it shall be a heap for ever, it shall not be built again.
>
> —Deuteronomy 13.12-16 (RSV)

Tantum religio potuit suadere malorum was Lucretius' (I, 101) inclusive formula: Religion keeps persuading people (men) to do all sorts of evil. Faced with a truth so patent that only a foaming-at-the-mouth fanatic would deny it, religious apologists will admit that, well, yes, every family has its black sheep. Jews will acknowledge that the biblical injunction of *herem*, aka ethnic cleansing or genocide, so exuberantly celebrated in the Book of Joshua, was horrific by modern, or any, standards. (The good news is that *herem* was almost certainly never carried out, not on the scale depicted in the Bible.) Catholics have no problem recognizing that burning, among other people, Joan of Arc at the stake in 1430 was a bad idea—and the Church itself decided to canonize her in 1920, a little late perhaps, but nonetheless a solid two-thumbs-up for a once-hated heretic. Protestants—whose history is shorter and who hence have less to regret—will likely shake their heads over Calvin's blessing the incineration of Michael Servetus in Geneva. And Christians of all persuasions are beginning to see the many downsides of the Crusades. Finally, most of today's Muslims are repelled by the Wahhabi-type targeting of innocent civilians. Killing men, women, and children in God's name and at his alleged invitation appears to be getting less popular than it once was (though killing animals with his express approval is still big, see Chapter Chapter Fourteen, "God Abuses Animals).

So, good for believers—some of them anyway. In any case, God can hardly be blamed for all the oceans of religious bloodshed if he doesn't exist, right? No doubt those rousing tales of wicked sinners whacked from on high (Sodom and Gomorrah! Pharaoh's charioteers! Korah, Dathan, and Abiram! Ananias and Sapphira! The Whore of Babylon! The tribes of 'Ad and Thamud [wiped out by Allah]!, etc.) were rooted in the hyperactive Semitic imagination, not history.

And so we can all breathe a sigh of relief. Except for what history tells us, which is that the very idea of God is poisonous; and his very name must be laid to rest for the sake of peace (not that godless humans can't and won't find other reasons for wholesale slaughter—male aggression generally does the trick). There's no reason, in principle, why fantasies of God couldn't promote peace, they just don't. On the other hand, how about a brief review of the bad news, alphabetically arranged? All this stuff is more or less familiar, but the disgusting ensemble it adds up to needs to be periodically reviewed.

Religious Violence, a Rapid Random Sampling

Albigensian Crusade (1209-1229)—the Catholic Church stamps out the Cathar heresy, killing perhaps as many as 1,000,000 people. A special feature was mass burnings of recalcitrant apostates. The world-famous *bon mot* of Arnaud Amalric at the siege of Béziers in 1209, when asked by a Crusader how to tell Catholics from Cathars, "Kill them all—God will know which ones are his" has been the subject of much controversy.

Anita Bryant (b. 1940)—Celebrated Christian homophobe: "If gays are granted rights, next we'll have to give rights to prostitutes and to people who sleep with St. Bernards." See Rick Santorum.

Another, less famous 1066-event—Fanatical Muslim Sanhaja Berbers assassinate hundreds of Cordova Jews.

Arab military conquests—Beginning in 622, the Middle East, North Africa, Spain, India, etc. witnessed Allah's holy warriors at their finest. Unhappy populations that resisted were occasionally slaughtered or enslaved or both.

Armenian genocide (1915-1917)—half to one and a half million people killed by the Turks, who no doubt found the task easier knowing that their victims were unbelievers.

Asma bint Marwan—satirical woman poet, murdered in 624 on orders from Muhammad, who lacked, among other things, a sense of humor.

Aurengzeb (1617-1708)—Champion Mughal persecutor of Hindus and Sikhs, led forced conversions to Islam, torturing and killing the recalcitrant.

Baha'is—persecuted and killed (200 +) by the Islamic Republic of Iran, barred from universities, their sacred sites destroyed, etc.

Blood Libel—a Christian spécialité, with masterful versions staged in Kishniev (1903) and Kielce (1946), killing scores of Jews. Iranian Muslims held a spirited blood libel pogrom in Shiraz (1910), marked by mass violence and depredations.

Bogdan Khmelnitsky—Ukrainian hetman who led the slaughter of tens of thousands of Jews from 1648 to 1656. He visited similar horrors on the Poles, who likewise differed from him in religion. There is a large monument to him in Kiev.

Book-burning—First instigated by the Christians of Ephesus (Acts 19.19), the beginning of a proud religious tradition.

Book of Joshua—the (most likely fictitous) story of bloodthirsty Israelite berserkers who carried out the first ethnic cleansing in Canaan, as God (not for the last time) blessed genocide.

Bosnian war (1992-1995)—100,000 people, mostly Muslims, killed by Christians

Giordano Bruno—Brilliant writer and proponent of heliocentrism, burned at the stake for heresy in Rome's Campo dei Fiori on February 17, 1600, in no small part thanks to the efforts of St. Robert Bellarmine, S.J., who once said that "in the dictionary of love you cannot find the word 'impossible'." Four hundred years later the Catholic Church apologized in another official papal "Oops."

Catholic martyrs under Elizabeth I—Estimates vary, perhaps as many as 312, which works out to a modest seven a year, as opposed to the 284 Protestants executed by Blood Mary Tudor (ca. 57 a year).

Christianization of the New World—A complicated process, since it was part of a larger economic, political, cultural, etc. campaign of domination. In n any case through disease (small pox, measles, typhus, diphtheria, etc., by no means always spread by accident) and violence, it destroyed something like 90% of all the natives unlucky enough to experience it. "Go ye, therefore, and teach all nations."

Clitoridectomies—130,000,000 and counting, mostly in African Muslim countries (but Coptic Christians are o.k. with the practice too) and endorsed by fatwas from Egypt's Al Azhar University, though the most recent one was issued in 1981—all part of the endless monotheistic campaign to confine and control female sexuality.

Cromwell in Ireland (1649-1652)—Padraig Lenihan in *Confederate Catholics at War* estimates that 15-20% of the population of Ireland was killed or exiled by the born-again Protestant crusader and his allies.

Crusades—Nearly two centuries (1095-1272) of God-blessed mayhem. No one knows how many millions of Muslims, Jews, and Christians, most of them civilians, were killed in the course of these nine Sacred Blood Baths, giving rise to a word that westerners somehow continue to use without blushing or apologizing.

Death penalty—Popular with all theistic traditions, especially Christianity and Islam, at least until recently. The Bible tells of Israelites killed for gathering sticks on the Sabbath (Numbers 15.36) and stealing booty from Jericho (Joshua 7.25). The Torah demands capital punishment for a wide variety of crimes, from disrespecting one's parents to getting married without a hymen. Jewish commentators stress the rarity with which such death sentences were carried out. The Southern Baptist Convention and other red-blooded, red-state Christian groups strongly support killing criminals.

English Reformation—Lunatic Puritans destroy Catholic churches, smash stained glass windows, "bare ruined choirs where late the sweet birds sang."

Expulsion of Jews and Muslims from Spain—1492 also marks the beginning of Spain's decay. The exact numbers will never be known, certainly in the hundreds of thousands, many of whom perished in the process. Enough were forced to convert so that today some 20% of Spaniards have Jewish genes (11% have Muslim ancestry). See Nicholas Wade, NYTimes, December 4, 2008, "Gene Test Shows Spain's Jewish and Muslim Mix."

Gayle Williams—Aid worker for Serve Afghanistan murdered by the Taliban for "preaching Christianity," October 20, 2008. Just one of many.

Holocaust—The 6,000,000 Jews murdered by the Nazis were not primarily victims of religious hatred, but the silence and collusion of Christian churches, clergy, and believers, played a part in their deaths, which had also been prepared for by 2,000 years of theologically flavored anti-Judaism and Jew-hatred.

Iconoclasm—All theomaniacs have done it, early Christians, Byzantines, Muslims, Protestants, etc. The bloodiest practitioners seem to have been the Byzantines, who in the 8th and 9th century assaulted the so-called iconodules. In the "Decade of Blood" (762-775) thousands of monks were killed for their supposed idolatry.

Jan Hus—Utterly decent Czech reformer, burnt to death by the Catholic Church on July 6, 1415.

Jedwabne—Poland, site of mass murders by devout Catholics of some 1,600 Jews on July 10, 1941. Most were burned alive.

Jews of Quraysh—In 627 the Banu Qurazya were (dubiously) accused of treason by Muhammad, who had 600-900 of their men beheaded (cf. Daniel Pearl) and their women and children enslaved. The Qur'an is saturated with anger at the Jews.

Leo Max Frank—Innocent Jew lynched by a mob of stalwart Georgia Christians on August 17, 1915. He has since been pardoned, but his name has not been cleared.

Lord's Resistance Army (LRA)—Ugandan movement with bases in Sudan, founded in 1987, led by deluded killer Joseph Kony, aims to set up a theocratic state grounded in the Ten Commandments, advances its cause through murder, rape, slavery, abduction of children, etc. No solid figures available for the number of victims to date.

Mansur Al-Hallaj—Persian mystic tortured and murdered in 922 for identifying himself with God. Allah does NOT like this sort of foolery.

Martin Luther—Who wrote so memorably, in *Of the Jews and Their Lies* (1543), that Jews were "full of the devil's feces . . . in which they wallow like swine." No Nazi could have said it better.

Mazar-i-Sharif (and Bamiyan) massacres—1998, Taliban slaughter over 8,000 suspected apostates and leave their corpses to rot in the sun.

Michael Servetus—Gifted Spanish physician and humanist burned at the stake in Geneva by John Calvin & Co. in 1553 for denying the Trinity and "paedobaptism."

Mormon Meadows Massacre—Righteous Latter Day Saints murdered 120 men, women, and children, in 1857 and have continued to deny it for a century and a half.

Northern Ireland—Site of the Protestant vs. Catholic "Troubles" since the 1960s, which resulted in the murder of over 3,000 people.

Old Believers—Russian Christian lunatics who rejected the liturgical reforms of Patriarch Nikon (1652-1658). For the unspeakable heresy of making the sign of the cross with two rather than three fingers and other such crimes, they were persecuted, tortured, and slain. Many responded by immolating themselves.

Oxford martyrs—Peddling insufficiently Catholic brands of God-talk led to the burning at the stake of Bishops Hugh Latimer, Nicholas Ridley (both on October 16, 1555), and Archbishop Thomas Cranmer (March 21, 1556). Membership in the clergy can be dangerous to your health.

Pilgrimage of Grace (1536-37)—216 Catholics whacked for protesting against Henry VIII's religious innovations.

Pius IX—Sent hundreds of troops to certain death to defend his Papal States in the battles of Castelfidardo (1860) and Porta Pia (1870). There was no chance of victory, but it's the thought that counts.

Pogroms—A constant feature of 19th and early 20th century Russian life, associated in particular with the revolutions of 1905 and 1917, with casualties in the hundreds of thousands. The good news is, the butchery drove many Jews to emigrate, thus lowering the numbers killed after the Nazi invasion of Russia in 1941. See Isaac Babel's "The Story of My Dovecot" and *Red Cavalry* passim.

Polygyny—Popular with theomanic patriarchs everywhere. Solomon may have set the record with 700 wives and 300 concubines (1 Kings 11.2), assuming the Bible wasn't fibbing. The great Jewish sage Maimonides (d. 1204) said a man could marry as many women as he could support. Muhammad Awad Bin Laden, Osama's father, supposedly had twenty-two wives. Tens of thousands of Mormons, mostly in Utah and Arizona, continue the tradition of Christian polygyny and wife-abuse in our day.

Pope Paul IV (reigned 155-1559)—Your basic Counter-Reformation monster. Created the Roman ghetto, where Jews were forced to live for the next three centuries, founded the Index of Fordbidden Books, and revived the Inquisition in Italy.

Prohibition—Passed mostly thanks to Protestan zealots, like Presbyterian minister Mark A. Matthews (d. 1940) who wrote: "The saloon is the most fiendish, corrupt, hell-soaked institution that ever crawled out of the slime of the eternal pit. . . . It takes your sweet innocent daughter, robs her of her virtue, and transforms her into a brazen, wanton harlot. . . . It is the open sore of this land."

Proposition 8 (November, 2008)—Mormons unite with other true believers to ban gay marriage in California.

Quakers—hanged in Massachusetts: 1659, William Robinson and Marmadule Stephenson, joined by Mary Dyer in 1660. True Christians *hate* heretics.

Rick Santorum—Devout Catholic homophobe. Quoted in *USA Today* (4/03/2003) as saying: "In every society, the definition of marriage has not ever to my knowledge included homosexuality. That's not to pick on homosexuality. It's not, you know, man on child, man on dog, or whatever the case may be."

Rwandan genocide—1994, Hutus from"the most Christian country in Africa" slaughter ca. 800,000 of their Tutsi compatriots, with Catholic clergy and nuns sometimes leading the way.

Saint Bartholomew's Day Massacre—Started in Paris on August 24, 1572. Something like 2,000 Huguenots were slaughtered in Paris, 3,000 in the provinces. Pope Gregory XIII had a *Te Deum* sung and a medal struck to commemorate the happy event.

Salafists—Muslim enthusiasts who think everything went seriously downhill after the first three generations of Islam. A famous modern representative is Sayyid Qutb (1906-1966), the current guru of Islamists everywhere. On a trip to the USA he was grossed out by the excesses of American individualism and the shameless lechery evident, for example, at a church dance in Greeley, Colorado. Ian Buruma and Avishai Margolit note in *Occidentalism* (2004) that "Qutb's idea of community is defined by pure faith, just as the Nazi state was based on pure race. 'Jewish agents' pollute the purity of these communities and must therefore be eradicated."

Salem witch trials (1692)—25 people judicially murdered by Christian maniacs. Seemed like a good idea at the time.

Slavery—No problem for Moses, St. Paul, or Muhammad. As 1 Peter 2.18 says, "Slaves (*oiketai*), be subject to your masters, with all fear, not only to the good and gentle but also to the froward." Slavery persists today in various parts of the Muslim world, e.g., Mauretania.

Spanish Inquisition (1478-1834)—Hypervigilant persecution of Marranos, Moriscos, and heretical scum of every description. Christian torture at its finest. Estimates of victims burned at the stake or otherwise murdered vary widely. Three thousand?

Srebrenica massacre of 1995—Serbian Orthodox Christians murder 8,000 Bosnian Muslim boys and men in a particularly thorough ethnic cleansing.

Sunni-Shia split—the world's longest running religious *casus belli*, with casualties running in the hundreds of thousands, and continually rising, thanks to the US invasion of Iraq. Apart from the well-known foundational dispute of the rightly-guided Caliphs vs. Ali, there are endless fascinating differences between the two groups, for example on the Shia practice of *mutah*, or the divinely blessed one-night stand (for husbands and their girlfriends, not wives with their boyfriends). Sunnis and Shias also oppress their women differently. See the wikipedia article on "Sunni-Shia relations."

Taliban—Mullah Omar and his "students": In the *NY Times* Nov. 22, 2001, Amy Waldman ("A Nation Challenged: The Law") writes: "A kite seller will be imprisoned for three days. The owner of a house will be punished if women are heard singing during a wedding. No images or photographs are to be posted in public places. The following are considered 'unclean things': 'pork, pig, pig oil, anything made from human hair, satellite dishes, cinematography, any equipment that produces the joy of music, pool tables, chess, masks, alcohol, tapes, computer, VCR's, televisions, anything that propagates sex and is full of music, wine, lobster, nail polish, firecrackers, statues, sewing catalogs, pictures, Christmas cards.'" Earlier generations of Jewish and Christian puritans would have drooled at the prospect.

Thirty Years War (1618-1648)—religiously-themed military and civilian holocaust in Central Europe, perhaps as many as seven and a half million killed. (The wolf population, however, soared.) See Bertolt Brecht's *Mother Courage*.

William Tyndale—The great Bible translator was hunted down, tried, and executed for heresy near Brussels in 1536. He was "mercifully" strangled before his corpse was burnt.

Wahhabis—Maniacal followers of Ibn 'Abd-al-Wahhab (1703-1792) who launched his righteous career by having an adulteress stoned to death. In 1802 his warriors attacked Karbala and massacred the population. Wahhabism is now the reigning religious insanity in Saudi Arabia, whence it gets exported all over the planet.

Waldensian massacres—Ca. 500 years of persecution of this peaceable Protestant sect by the Holy Roman Caholic Church and its agents, which included the burning to death of 80 or more Waldensian heretics in Strasbourg, the 1487 crusade against French Waldensians, which wiped them out, and the 1655 massacre by the Duke of Savoy of Waldensians in northern Italy.

Witchcraft trials—Nobody knows how many thousands of people have been tried and executed as witches in Europe over the centuries. Figures range from about 12,000 upwards to (an unlikely) 100,000, all with the full support of Christian churches. (Exodus 22.18 "Thou shall not suffer a witch to live.") In our time the murder of witches is a popular blood sport in Africa. See Frank Bures, "A Mind Dismembered: In search of the magical penis thieves," *Harpers* June, 2008. Sarah Palin's former pastor Thomas Muthee is an accomplished witch-hunter.

Chapter Ten

God the Father—and the Perils of Permanent Puerility

> But now, O LORD, thou art our father:
>
> —Isaiah 64.8

> But what about other men and women who have been raised in a sensible fashion? Perhaps the ones who don't suffer from the neurosis [of religion] won't need any intoxicant to anesthetize it. To be sure, they'll find themselves in a difficult position. They'll have to admit to themselves just how helpless they are and how insignificant a cog in the machinery of the universe. No longer can they be the center of creation, the focus of a kindly Providence's tender care. Their situation will be just like that of a child who has left the home of its parents where life was so warm and cozy. But surely childish ways are meant to be overcome. People can't remain children forever. Eventually they have to make their way out into "hostile life." We could call this "reality education."
>
> —Sigmund Freud, *The Future of an Illusion* (1927)

Nobody ever said that giving up God for dead—much less participating, at least passively, in his murder—was going to be easy. That, once again, was the madman's point in *The Gay Science*. If being godless were seen as a positive condition like drug-free or dry and sober, there would be therapeutic programs for recovering believers all over the country. But theism is a socially approved addiction : There was scarcely a peep of protest after the All Star Home Run Derby on July 14,

2008 when ESPN newscaster Rick Reilly, gloating over born-again slugger Josh Hamilton's 28 first-round dingers, exclaimed, "It's a lousy day to be an atheist!" (Alas, Hamilton, a former alcoholic and junkie, lost in the final round to the less devout Justin Morneau.) And we all know there are no atheists in foxholes (except maybe in the Chinese Civil War).

Ex-believers are given nasty names like apostate, heretic, renegade, backslider, defector, fallen-away, and the like. Things would be different if we equated godlessness with heroic acts of self-discipline like overcoming a disability or kicking a bad habit. And belief is in some ways as much a biochemical dependency (on chanting, prostrating, incense-burning, memorizing magic formulas, eating sacred foods, wearing holy garments, etc.) as a philosophical-psychological one. Alternately, imagine if we compared casting off belief—as Freud implicitly does—to getting weaned or toilet-trained, to dressing oneself or learning to read and write. It's all in the metaphors.

Freud, of course, lived in an age even more patriarchal than ours; so he laid a lot of stress on the Divine Father figure and getting over him. But it still makes perfect sense to attack The Big Guy (dead as he is and dangerous as it is to say so). The laws of developmental psychology can't be trampled on with impunity: Adults have to cut loose from their parents, or they're not adults. Autonomy and unquestioning obedience (adoration, subordination, dedication, etc.) are forever incompatible. The correct answer for Abraham to God's order to take Isaac to the land of Moriah and slaughter him there as a burnt offering (Genesis 22.2) would have been: "Are you out of your fucking mind?"

Even if God's commands were always morally correct (which they're not—executing adulterers, for example, is a horrible idea), we couldn't just sit there and take them. (See Chapter Six, "Don't Do as God Says—or as He Does"). Grownups have to think and act responsibly for themselves. That doesn't mean, by the way, that unaided human efforts are enough to make life safe or even bearable: One of the reasons adulthood is difficult is that adults realize their power and control have narrow limits, and the only place they can look for help is from other similarly handicapped humans.

The problem of authority-and-rebellion has concerned men (Oedipus and all that) more than women; but that was because of sexism. Everybody, female and male, has to break free from the clutches of God (and his shoddy imitators on earth); and it will have escaped nobody's notice that the majority of the people in churches (though not in synagogues and mosques—Christianity is more feminine-friendly) at any given time are likely to be women. Banned from being movers and shakers for God, they became the moved and the shaken; and, as always, religious indoctrination helps to keep the ladies in line outside the sacred precincts. For this very reason, for all the damage done to women in the name of God from Moses' consigning them to the status of property ("Thou shalt not covet thy neighbour's house, thou shalt not covet thy neighbor's wife, nor his manservant nor his maidservant, nor his ox, nor his ass, nor anything that is thy neighbor's" (Exodus 19.17) to Paul's condemning them to permanent inferiority ("The head of the woman is the man," 1 Corinthians 11.3) to Muhammad's unblushing misogyny ("Men have authority over women because God has made the one superior to the other, and because they spend their wealth to maintain them," 4:34), from clericalism to clitoridectomy, women have every reason to hate God and want him dead. Arguing that all we need to do is prune God of a few noxious excrescences that men have slapped onto him won't help, any more than photoshopping an old portrait of Grandpa to fix his teeth, update his wardrobe, and put a smile on his stolid, frozen face.

But, overwhelming as the case is against the repulsive figure that William Blake called "Nobodaddy" (see Chapter Thirteen "God the Bully: Sic Semper Tyrannis"), even Freud would have to admit that not all believers' associations with the Divine Dominator need be negative. Whenever you get so many humans involved for so long a time in creating a God and a system for worshiping him, you're bound to come up with a few positive, life-enhancing features (perhaps like the poison curare). Most notably, belief in an imaginary Father provides an occasion for liturgical get-togethers, with song, story, solemn choreography, and (often best of all) socializing afterwards. In a disjointed, alienated world this creates a sense of community not readily obtainable elsewhere. Truth be told, there's little doubt that a hefty minority, at least, of worshipers are actually agnostics along for the convivial ride (no harm in that), just as some Jewish atheists keep kosher.

But for the sake of their mental health, believers need to break the theological ties that bind. Among the symptoms of theistic childishness are resignation to the status quo ("Let every soul be subject unto the higher powers: for there is no power but of God. The powers that be are ordained of God," Romans 13.1), postponement of pleasure ("For all that is in the world, the lust of the flesh, the lust of the eyes, and the pride of life, is not of the Father, but is of the world. And the world passeth away and the lust thereof," 1 John 2.16-17), self-contempt ("When ye shall have done all those things which are commanded you, say, 'We are unprofitable servants'" Luke 17.19), a propensity to blind obedience ("And he [Moses]said unto them, 'Thus saith the LORD God of Israel. "Put every man his sword by his side, and go in and out from gate to gate throughout the camp, and slay every man his brother, and every man his companion, and every man his neighbour."' And the children of Levi did according to the word of Moses" (Exodus 32.27-28), and many other forms of dysfunctional thought and behavior.

Anyone thinking about God the Father (with or without a Son) needs to steer clear of modern touchy-feely notions of paternity and recall the much tougher family culture of biblical times. In Genesis 19 when his house was besieged by the gay mob in Sodom, Lot offered his virgin daughters to be gang-raped, rather than violate his obligation to his angelic guests. Abraham, as mentioned, had no objection, in principle, to killing his son at Yahweh's behest. Jephthah went right ahead and slew his nameless daughter to fulfill a vow to the LORD (she herself took her murder in stride). Any child who cursed his or her parents was supposed to be stoned to death (Lev. 20.). Sons who are drunken, gluttonous, stubborn and rebellious are likewise to be lapidated (Deut. 21.21). The Book of Proverbs (23.13-14), as we all know, recommends shellacking children: "Withhold no correction from the child: for if thou beatest him with the rod, he shall not die. Thou shalt beat him with the rod, and shalt deliver his soul from hell."

From almost every angle the whole divine-father-metaphor looks lame. We've all heard of large families, but six-plus billion kids (and counting, not to mention the dead)? No wonder he has so little quality-time to spend on each of us. And how much of our Daddy's DNA do we share anyway? Next to none, to judge by appearances. Why would he or we want to share each other's company? How deep would believers' disappointment go if they were told, "Look, you can have anything your heart desires for as long as you want; but you won't ever literally meet God"? Mystics may voice their longing to get up-close and personal with God, along the lines of Psalm 42.1-2, "As the hart panteth after the water brooks, so panteth my soul after thee,) God. My soul thirsteth for God, for the living God: when shall I come and appear before God?" But, apart from the rarity of such yearnings, what they really express is doubt and impatience ("Where the hell *is* he?")

God the Father—and the Perils of Permanent Puerility 69

All relationships are by definition two-way streets; but we can't give anything to our Trillionaire Papa who already has it all. He may want praise, worship, or a gold-star moral report card from us; but that's for *our* benefit, not his. He doesn't need a single thing that's in our capacity to bestow, though he might out of sheer kindness agree to go along with the parental charade of surprise and delight at our feeble miniature presents. Scripture may depict him as furiously angry over our transgressions; but that's got to be poetic license: The Master of the Universe must by definition be invulnerable. If God ever had a theme song, it would have to be, *mutatis mutandis*, Royce Da 5' 9"'s "Can't Touch Me." But, as always, why bother with Someone you can't touch?

Real fathers are often as violent as—though infinitely less powerful than—the Lord of Hosts . But they themselves are all part of a vast chain of relatives, from their mates to their parents and siblings and so on; whereas our Divine Father towers over the masses on planet earth in his eerie, chilling uniqueness. "To whom then will you compare me," the Holy One shouts in Isaiah 40.25 (RSV), "that I should be like him?" Nobody, Lord, nobody! You dah Man!

By way of bidding farewell to the Old One, we might review the most famous Christian prayer, the Our Father (although if they hadn't been snakebit by centuries of hatred and persecution, Jews might have adopted it too, since it contains no references whatsoever to Christ, even though Jesus is said to have invented it). Here it is in the New Revised Standard Version (Matthew 6.9-13):

Our Father in heaven (the usual problem: he's somewhere far far away, not here where he's needed)

hallowed be your name. (a glutton for glorification, as always—does he have an inferiority complex?)

Your kingdom come, (but he always keeps us waiting, doesn't he? Why can't he *make* it come?)

your will be done, on earth as it is in heaven (dream on—never the twain shall meet).

Give us this day our daily bread	(i.e., "bread for tomorrow," the never-to-be-served messianic banquet)
And forgive us our debts, as we also have forgiven our debtors.	(sorry, all accounts are payable only on terra firma, not up in the sky)
And do not bring us into temptation,	(why would he want to do *that*? What kind of s.o.b. Is he?)
but rescue us from the evil one.	(Sheesh, not *him* again? Humans aren't bad enough, they have to be aided and abetted in their wickedness by an imaginary Super-Villain?)
For the kingdom and power and glory are yours forever. Amen.	(Rah-rah-rah, sis-boom-ba.)

It's time, as St. Paul himself said, to put away childish things (1 Corinthians 13.11), including Yahweh-Allah. What's cute in pre-school gets really embarrassing in grad school.

Chapter Eleven

Your God's Too Big

> I am here obliged to vindicate the reputation of an excellent lady, who was an innocent sufferer upon my account. The Treasurer took a fancy to be jealous of his wife, from the malice of some evil tongues, who informed him that her Grace had taken a violent affection for my person., and the court scandal ran for some time, that she once came privately to my lodging. This I solemnly declare to be a most infamous falsehood, without any grounds, farther than that her Grace was pleased to treat me with all innocent marks of freedom and friendship.
>
> —Swift, *Gulliver's Travels*, Part One, Chapter VI

Among the many sexual jokes in *Gulliver's Travels* are the size-matters capriccios. Young soldiers in the army of Lilliput are overcome with "laughter and admiration" at the sight of Gulliver's genitals (his body-mass is 1728 times greater than theirs) as they march between his outstretched legs and gaze up through the crotch of his tattered breeches. When the tables are turned in Brobdingnag, Gulliver seems—despite his protests to the contrary—to be more than a little titillated by the heroic proportions of the naked giantesses who play with him ("The handsomest among these Maids of Honour, a pleasant frolicsome girl of sixteen, would sometimes set me astride one of her nipples, with many other tricks, where in the reader will excuse me for not being over particular.")

The point of the story about "her Grace" in Lilliput is, of course, that Gulliver's supposed inamorata was less than five inches high; so the chances of her finding any relief for her "violent affection" were drastically limited. (Impossible discrepancies in size enable Gulliver to enjoy piquant arousal without the need for actual coitus, which Swift himself seems to have eschewed). All of this can serve as a satirical illustration of the problems facing human love for God, who, if he existed, would obviously be too big. Holy Writ is forever crowing about the greatness of Yahweh ("Who is so great a God as our God?" asks Psalm 77.13, without waiting for a response); and Muslims continuously clamor that their God is great too.

There's no gainsaying that biblical evocations of such divine grandeur can at times be truly, er, grand. Consider the sensational conclusion to the prophecies of Second Isaiah, where God seizes the mike and declares: "For my thought are not your thoughts, neither are your ways my ways, saith the LORD. For as the heavens are higher than the earth, so are my ways higher than your ways, and my thoughts than your thoughts. For as the rain cometh down, and the snow from heaven, and returneth not thither, but watereth the earth, and maketh it bring forth and bud, that it may give seed to the sower, and bread to the eater: so shall my word be that goeth forth out of my mouth: it shall not return unto me void, but it shall accomplish that which I please, and it shall prosper in the thing whereto I sent it" (55.8-10). Wow (really). Across the globe there aren't many things bigger than the hydrological cycle; and Gods don't come much greater than Second Isaiah's. But suppose "great" translated to absolutely incompatible?

No doubt this sounds too simple-minded, but that's mostly because canned-theistic, rather than impromptu-atheistic, discourse is the norm for public speech. So perhaps the God-talking bias could be broken down by asking a few easy (to ask, not to answer) questions: Since all the theologians agree that God is infinite, and everything else, including us, is finite, how could there be any meaningful relationship between humans and the deity? We have pet animals (not insects, though, apart from the odd tarantula) and we love wild flora and fauna; but "pet rocks" are at best a tedious gag; and so, it seems, would be the notion of an infinite Being having pet persons.

This problem isn't too acute in the Bible and the Qur'an, because their authors represent God rather loosely as "someone" who is both huge, yet down-to-earth. The LORD strolls through the garden of Eden like any other suburban homeowner. When he speaks to his prophets, God conveniently addresses them in their native tongue, like any normal human "caller." This modestly-dimensioned God, one might say, is manageable. (In fact, the Bible in Daniel 3.1 makes fun of super-colossal false deities, in the ninety-foot tall golden statue of Nebuchadnezzar supposedly erected on the plain of Dura.) But when theologians begin to reflect on what it all means, on what "conditions of possibility" would have to obtain for the glorious Being described in Holy Writ to do business, problems arise.

God in the Bible may sometimes sound fallible, as when in Genesis 6.6 he regrets creating the human race or again in Genesis 8.22 when he realizes that the Flood was a mistake (because sin-prone humans can't help themselves). But the God-talkers inform us that the LORD is all-knowing, all-wise, all-powerful, all-good, all-everything. If he weren't all those wonderful things and more—infinitely patient, compassionate, and just—then he wouldn't be, you know, *special*. And if he weren't special, well, what kind of a God would he be?

Sadly, these supernal absolutes don't jibe with either lived experience or even the text of the Bible. But they're needed as shock-absorbers for scenes like the one in Exodus 6.24 where Yahweh tries to kill Moses because he forgot to get circumcised (a curious oversight, no?), or that weird episode in Mark 5.18 when Jesus masterminds the drowning of 2,000 perfectly healthy and very valuable swine (sue the bastard!). Or, more to the point, the countless unbearable moments or eras, of personal or group or species history that call into question the existence or helpfulness of the Supreme Being. (See Chapter Eight, "God Falling Short? Extrapolate! Extrapolate!")

We know the theodicean drill: Things may *look* bad (as they did, for example, to Job after Satan carried out his divinely licensed devastation of Job's life); but that's only because we can't see the Big Picture. (Older readers may recall the homiletic chestnut of comparing "this life" to the reverse side of a tapestry, all knotted and ugly—whereas in the new and improved second life we'll finally get to see the gorgeous, variegated, flawless, etc. pattern executed by the Divine Weaver. So stop complaining.)

Which brings us back to the unbridgeable asymmetry between God and his creatures. If he's got the whole world in his hands, then how do we deal with divine digits that span billions of light years? God-talkers assure us that he can simultaneously listen to the music of the spheres *and* auscultate the inner organs of over six billion humans (plus the beasts)—but how boring would that be? Why bother?

On the other hand, why should *we* waste any time with *him* (apart from perhaps fearing the pain he might inflict on us)? Aren't we satisfied with the various life forms and natural beauties we encounter on planet earth? Does anyone, except for psychotics, really need more than the company of humans, animals, plants, and some select kinds of inanimate matter? Do we feel an unquenchable innate longing for some sort of ecological niche (heaven) that transcends all the ones we've already seen? Many, if not most, of us would like to have a lot more of this world's pleasures, without its painful limitations and deprivations; but that's not infinity.

Beyond not wanting or needing contact with the Cosmic Número Uno, mightn't we just hate it? Wouldn't it be way too much information for our tiny, fragile hard drives? How could we be ourselves whilst overshadowed by that humongous storm cloud? No doubt, some people would enjoy dating, or mating with, someone far out of their league, but not *that* far out. What could a couple like that ever talk about? Alternately, God could shrink himself or dumb himself down, (which must be what happens in the Bible and the Qur'an) so that we could grasp him without feeling overwhelmed; but then how would he be God? If God is "totally other," as Karl Barth said about the deity we meet in Paul's Letter to the Romans, wouldn't we by definition find his presence alienating (and vice versa)?

Unless one is a lunatic Platonist like St. Augustine, it's hard to understand the spiritual passion (see Chapter Seven, "God Is Spirit—But What's That?") felt by God's self-proclaimed lovers. "What do I love," asked the bishop of Hippo, "whenas I love thee? Not the beauty of any corporal thing; nor the order of times, nor the brightness of the light, which we do behold, so gladsome to the eyes: not the pleasant melodies of songs of all kinds; nor the fragrant smell of flowers, and ointment, and spices; not manna and honey; nor any fair limbs that are so acceptable to fleshly embracements. I love none of these things whenas I love my God" (*Confessions* X, 6, tr. William Watts, 1631). Having totally disembodied God (as Christian dogma obliged him to) and come up with a God unsullied by any physical things, Augustine nonetheless insists that God mysteriously communicates a much sublimer version of those good things through humans' outer senses to their "inner man."

Could be, but wouldn't a likelier reading of this claim be that Augustine was in fact using his well-known sensory susceptibility as a launching pad, or diving board, for flights or plunges into an imaginary territory called, for lack of a better word, God? Significantly, even flesh-hating Augustine couldn't quite reach escape velocity (no one can); and so he admits that in loving God he loves "*a certain kind* of light, and a *kind* of voice, and a *kind* of fragrance, and a *kind* of meat [food], and a *kind* of embracement"—all "interior" kinds, of course, not the shabby, grungy, icky, superficial, external stuff. Sure, sure—but Augustine makes a fine hostile witness for the prosecution of God.

The Lord may technically be infinite, but in fact he has to be cut down to size to be dealt with. Otherwise, he's just too big. But then, once reduced to our own proportions, isn't he just a fanciful amalgam of all the good things we've seen or dreamed of in our own purely down-to-earth moments? And in that case, why not opt for the real (totally terrestrial) McCoy? When he got home from the giant-world of Brobdingnag, Gulliver had a hard time adjusting to the picayune proportions of his fellow Brits—but by that point he had already started to get a little crazy (life will do that to you); and most of us would be happy to settle down for the long haul with other members of our own species, however modestly sized. The Big Fella is just too big.

Chapter Twelve

God the Bully: Sic Semper Tyrannis

> I saw the Lord standing upon the altar; and he said,
> "Smite the lintel of the door, that the posts may shake:
> and cut them in the head, all of them,
> and I will slay the last of them with the sword:
> he that fleeth of them shall not flee away,
> and he that escapeth of them shall not be delivered.
> Though they dig into hell,
> thence shall my hand take them:
> though they climb up to heaven,
> thence will I bring them down: . . .
> and though they be hid from my sight in the bottom of the sea,
> thence will I command the serpent, and he shall bite them.
> And though they go into captivity before their enemies,
> thence will I command the sword, and it shall slay them:
> and I will set my eyes upon them, for evil and not for good."
>
> —Amos 9.1-4

> We [Allah] shall say: "Lay hold of him and bind him.
> Burn him in the fire of Hell, then fasten him with a chain seventy cubits long.
> For he did not believe in God, the Most Great, nor did he care to feed the destitute.
> Today he shall be friendless here, only filth shall be his food,
> the filth which only sinners eat.
>
> —Qur'an 69:30-37

God deserved to die above all because he was a bully. As George Daacon said, "If absolute power corrupts absolutely, where does that leave God?" And God's absolute power extended—still extends, when people let it—across so vast a spectrum from physical to mental to moral domination that it has to be rated the worst tyranny ever. Two obvious qustions are, why does he have to hog all the power to himself, and why can't he exercise it more gently?

With infinite power at his disposal, God has been signally stingy. He could in theory have been an Intelligent Designer; but he let the "blind watchmaker" of evolution fumble its way along for billions of years, with the overwhelming majority of species going extinct and individuals serving as disposable grist for the mills of natural selection. He could have shared far more of his infinite godly wisdom with his poor, unwitting creatures—but he didn't. So now we have the oft-noted paradox that within a couple of centuries humans have managed to raise their once feeble destructive capacity to a quasi-divine level—while having only token amounts of intelligence to manage it with.

In other words, we have a bunch of musclebound babies playing with nuclear warheads. Perhaps it pleased His Hyper-Intellectuality—not otherwise known for a sense of humor—to amuse himself with the round-the-clock vaudeville routine of trial-and-error (mostly error) afforded by his clueless children groping down the path to annihilation.

But, assuming that he had his reasons for withholding all but a smidgin of his superabundant brain-power (for lack of a more technical term), it's still hard not to take offense at the way he treats the offspring he has deprived of it. For example, take the ludicrous speech by God the Father in *Paradise Lost*, which he lambastes human beings (in advance) for being suckered by Satan. ("For man will hearken to his glozing lies,/ And easily transgress the sole command,/ Sole pledge of his obedience: so will fall/ He and his faithless progeny: whose fault?/ Whose but his own? Ingrate he had of me?/ All he could have; I made him just and right," III, 93-98). Of course, the whole idea of bringing God out onto the stage in person and then transcribing his *ipsissima verba* is a stunner. Earth to Milton: This is the late 17th century, man. The Royal Society has already been founded (1660). We live in a Copernican universe. New critical approaches to the Bible (Baruch Spinoza, Richard Simon, John Locke) are already looming. How can you expect to graft your quirky Calvinist cactus onto an Israelitish palm tree?

But Milton was simply falling back on tried-and-untrue theodicy when he attempted to wriggle out of the dilemma posed almost two millennia before by Epicurus: Either God has the power to help us or he doesn't. If he has it and doesn't want to use it (and where do we see any proof of his helpfulness?), then he's diabolically cruel. If he doesn't have the power, then by definition he's pathetically impotent, so why pay any heed to him? Now there's no intrinsic contradiction in God's being either cruel or (partly) impotent; it just wouldn't square with what the God-talkers have been telling us for millennia. We'd have to go back to some unthinkable theological drawing board. Much simpler to just bag the whole business.

Milton's hoary old excuse—that God desn't want us to be evil-proof, because he won't accept anything less than our freely offered obeisance—has all the solidity of a spider web; only it's not so attractive. If the price of freedom is such a titanic welter of misery, who wants to be free? Who would ever design a machine *not* to perform smoothly and effectively, but to go haywire and self-destruct? On the other hand, if we had to be free, why do we have so little actual freedom, with genes and circumstances more or less programming our every move? Was God such an egotist that he wouldn't settle for anything less than freely chosen loyalty-cum-hosannahs from his tiny creatures?

And what of this "hell" that Christians and Muslims keep chattering about? What's your favorite image: Gustave Doré 's dark abysses and writhing muscular wretches?The older, more colorful Hells of Hans Memling, Hieronymus Bosch, or Pieter Brueghel the Elder (The Fall of the Rebel Angels)? The most familiar write-ups of Hell, by Dante, Milton, Ignatius Loyola, Jonathan Edwards, et al, are all stirring in various ways, but philosophically insane. What kind of vengeful jollies is God supposed to be getting from his perfectly useless punishment (since once you're damned, it's too late to repent or make any reparation), for all eternity, of a motley collection of criminals, losers, and "sinners" in general? What an absurd waste. What were the theomavens (Christians and Muslims mostly) who invented Hell thinking when they rhapsodized about those undying fires, that unending agony? There's got to be a limit to Gotcha.

Alas, the obvious psychological explanation lies ready to hand: Frustrated, as many of us are, by the blatant failures of the human justice system, theistic seers dream of the ultimate Avenger, a divine Terminator, to clean things up once and for all. Naturally that can't be accomplished without slamming the brakes on the cursed wheel of history—as by the coming of the Messiah and the launching of the Last Judgment. Otherwise, even after the most thorough purgation and punishment, new evildoers will set to work again; and, like wolves with God's flock, begin new depredations. So, let's end this nonsense once and for all. Let's multiply the merits of the good and the guilt of the wicked by infinity (impossible to imagine that, but anything less would be coddling criminals and trivializing crime). It may be taking a pile driver to a mosquito, but it gives a paroxysmic sense of closure (see Chapter Nineteen, "God Closes the Deal").

And to achieve all this, the prophets and their followers need a really Big Bully, the righteousness of whose judgments can no more be questioned than the volcanic eruptions of his rage can be tamped down. You can't fight him, much less defeat him; and, as Job learned, you can't even argue with him (judge, jury, prosecutor, bailiff, court reporter—the Lord does just about everything, though he outsources the torture to Satan). The Bully knows all the answers, but he's not telling anybody else.

This maniacal monopoly of power must strike any fair-minded person as intolerable. By the right of primogeniture, so to speak, God gets to control the whole show. Those he condemns and those he forgives and blesses are equally dependent upon him, equally incapable of criticizing or second-guessing him. "For who hath known the mind of the Lord? Or who hath been his counsellor?" (Romans 11:34). "Hath not the potter power over the clay, of the same lump to make one vessel unto honour, and another unto dishonor?" (Rom. 9.21). Yahweh (Isaiah 64.8) and Allah (Qur'an 16:23) are both potters, and we're their clay—a frail and friable element, once it's been baked, as the Bible (Psalm 2.9, etc.) likes to remind us. Now that may sound like a dismal sort of relationship, from our standpoint at least; but since the nature of God is literally ineffable, believers—and, more importantly, God's spokesmen—have to stammer away as best they can.

Unfortunately, while God inhabits a timeless eternity, we humans are time-bound; and this makes all the authoritarian metaphors of the Bible and the Qur'an particularly grating. Back in ancient Israel or 7th century Arabia folks were comfortable with monarchy—and with images of God as one such monarch. But we aren't. A long political evolution has led us to democratically flattened views of power. God knows, democratic office-holders, with or without a real mandate, have done plenty of damage; but for all that, the rhetoric and imagery of government have changed forever. Even caudillos like Hugo Chávez have to act like regular guys. No emperors or caliphs for us: We've seen, if only on newsreels, too many versions of Big Brother staring down from banners and posters. Christ the King may tower in splendor over Rio de Janeiro and, by extension, all of the New World; but that's just theological kitsch, like its political counterparts on Mount Rushmore. Giant statues are out, except for the brain-dead votaries of Kim Il Sung and his ilk. When God gets too big for his britches and starts to terrorize everybody, we do what you always do to classroom bullies: give them some serious quiet time— in this case forever.

Chapter Thirteen

Divine Megalomania—It's Catching

> Behold, the nations are as a drop of a bucket, and are counted as the small dust of the balance: behold, he taketh up the isles as a very little thing. And Lebanon is not sufficient to burn, nor the beasts thereof sufficient for a burnt offering. All nations before him are as nothing; and they are counted to him less than nothing, and vanity.
>
> —Isaiah 40.15-17

> And we know that all things work together for good to them that love God, to them who are the called according to his purpose. For whom he did foreknow, he also did predestinate to be conformed to the image of his Son, that he might be the firstborn among many brethren. Moreover whom he did predestinate, them he also called: and whom he called, them he also justified: and whom he justified, them he also glorified. What shall we then say to these things? If God be for us, who can be against us?
>
> —Romans 8.28-31

As we've seen, God had to be gotten rid of because he was, among other things, an unbearable bully and braggart. A rapid glance at any of his numerous thar-she-blows fulgurations, fulminations, and fabrications in the Bible and the Qur'an will establish *that*. It seems the only way that monotheists could imagine the deity was by multiplying everything they thought of as grand to the nth degree, and then calling it God. This operation might be seen as a naive mistake, a poetic dream or a childish projection gone wild, and it is all that. But the supercolossal figure thus invented has to earn his keep. The vague deistic God on our currency may not be a high-maintenance guy (a nod in his direction at inaugurations, college commencements, and other official occasions will do the trick); but hard-core believers are required to spend quality time in supplication, flattery, ritual posturing, and various churchy doings if they expect to win and maintain divine favor.

The good news is, this outlay gets handsomely repaid: God serves as the supreme manifestation and guarantee of our own importance (what extraordinary kids we must be to have a Sitter this grand). This is crucial, because all the empirical evidence suggests that we—together with everything else in the universe—are no big deal. Infinitesimally small, constantly changing, short-lived, feeble, more or less erased forever at death, what's there to boast about? *Tout passe, tout casse, tout lasse.* Won't entropy and oblivion have the last word?

But then along comes Psalm 8, verse 5 claiming that God has made us only a little lower than himself and crowned us with "glory and honor." How cool is *that*! Yes, there are other Psalm verses (90.5) reminding us that we're nothing but grass, here today and gone tomorrow, and that in these decadent times we're doomed to live no more than 70 or 80 years. But such calls for humility are just ballast to prevent us from being swept away by our theological amour propre: We are after all God's creation, his beloved children, his pride and joy (on good days at least), and the object of his continuous attention. Ergo, all that depressing proof of our ontological insigificance can be overriden. *Wunderbar.*

Perhaps the best part of this rapturous religious dance is the way believers aggrandize themselves by groveling in guilty self-abasement before the Almighty. "All have sinned and come short of the glory of God,Through my fault, through my fault, through my most grievous fault, Domine, non sum dignus, Kyrie Eleison, I was shapen in iniquity, and in sin did my mother conceive me," yadda-yadda-yadda. Christians, of course, win the prize in this ditzy game of auto-humiliation: WE are SO AWFUL that GOD HIMSELF had to come down and FIX EVERYTHING. But HE DID! He joined our club, so we could join his. A round of applause for everybody.

What we have here is narcissism and nonsense fusing into perfect storm of religiosity. And it's all sanctioned by genetic programming. First of all, we have no choice but to see everything egocentrically. Not only is generic man (*anthropos*) the measure of all things; but so are all we individuals. We assume that the ceaselessly mutating atoms and impulses in *homines sapientes* (us!) somehow raises them to a mystical identity known as personhood; and we think perforce that our personal destiny is the most crucial thing in the universe. We may swat flies and mosquitos without a second thought (even as we dine on dead animals every day); but the prospect of *our* extinction is at once horrible and inconceivable. So what more plausible notion than that some Heavenly Power knows and cares about our precious—and gravely threatened—existence? If our parents worried about our every childhood bump, bruise, and fever, how could there not be a Divine Daddy to take care of us when we shuffle off this mortal coil? (See Chapter Ten, "God the Father—and the Perils of Permanent Puerility.")

As Paul Bloom argues in "Is God an Accident?" (*Atlantic,* December, 2005), children—and how many humans leave childish thinking behind?—can't help seeing purpose everywhere. Kids will say, for example, that lions are "meant" to be captured and put on display in zoos, for our amusement and delight. (Some fundamentalists seem to think the same is true of women.) No wonder Genesis shows all the animals trooping up in front of Adam to be named, catalogued, and placed at his disposition. That's what we do with all the stuff in our mental and physical worlds. Any creature that didn't see itself as the center of everything would never survive natural selection.)

But, alas, life and nature, with only minor exceptions, developed quite independently of us. They have no purpose; they just happened; and hence at bottom they couldn't care less about us. Of course, for the busy human brain *that* will never do. We can't handle chaos and randomness. We find it all but impossible not to construe nature as, at the very least, a spectacle staged for our benefit (as well as in some cases—cancer , cobras, hurricanes, etc.—for our destruction, though that provides dramatic spice). And how could there be a spectacle without a Producer-Director-M.C.? True, even with such anthropocentric assumptions, it's hard to draw a clear (not to mention appealing) picture of the Invisible Man in Charge from the muddled data of experience—but that's where God-talk comes in. Theologians wrote the book on how to tell tall tales.

Like a gigantically expanded cycle of Santa Claus stories, the myths, legends, images of God, along with pious lucubrations thereon, are presented by adults to children and young people, who are as a rule only too ready to accept these (mostly) comforting illusions. It all "makes sense": We *know* what precious little, or not-so-little, bundles we are. It would be nice to think that our parents, when they were copulating without contracepting, wanted to have us, at least in a general way. Even so, they couldn't possibly have known what the eventual collision between sperm and egg was going to lead to. But that still leaves open the gratifying scenario—as inculcated in youngsters by their *bien pensant* elders—that we were *personally*, from all eternity, a gleam in God's eye. And, having thus kept us in sight alll that time, how could he ever lose track of us? To be sure, the hassles of monitoring and, where appropriate, blessing and protecting and making post-mortem arrangements for the many billions of us, must beggar description. But, then, that's why he's God and we're not.

And that's why believers feel justified in attributing to him an array of qualities with no parallel, analogy, likeness, etc. whatsoever anywhere, ever. God, they say, has no material dimensions, never changes, is subject to no limits or constraints—which would seem to make him, paradoxically, useless for all pratical purposes (see Chapter Eleven, "Your God's Too Big"). But then comes the good news: he's a person, albeit a supercalifragilisticexpialodocious one. Thanks to that handy feature, believers can "relate" to him ("him" again), and, above all, talk to and about him.

One might object that this process of putting us, so to speak, in God's league could only be accomplished by cutting him to size; but that's not how the believers see it. (Forget for the moment the Christian dilemma of explaining how a few pints of blood shed by an ordinary-looking man who had once been a baby like everyone else could somehow save the entire planet.) God's unspeakable—well, semi-unspeakable—greatness winds up certifying *our* much less obvious greatness. If he's a mighty fortress, we must be somewhat rocklike ourselves. It's a mutual admiration society, with the Bible continually bidding believers to be holy as their God is holy (and being holy is, in the end, the only thing that matters, though holiness itself is devilishly hard to define). "Ye are a chosen generation," intones 1 Peter 2.9, "a royal priesthood, a holy nation, a peculiar [i.e., God's very special] people." Thanks to their imaginary Rich Uncle, all believers are virtual Croesuses. Jews, Christians, and Muslims wouldn't have it any other way.

Apart from the logical nonsense of constructing a Supernatural Entity out of thin air (at least Yahweh used an actual mudpie in Genesis 2 to create Adam), this splendiferousness-by-association is in really bad taste. We can't escape our modest animal status; and we shouldn't try or pretend to. Even as comic books and TV shows about Superman used to prompt foolish little boys to don capes and leap off high windowsills, so the God delusion has motivated countless Icarian flights into the make-believe stratosphere of our divine image-and-likeness. The theological astronauts don't crash and burn physically, but their sanity and honesty never remain altogether intact. Which is just one more reason for burying the corpse of divinity in the deepest grave possible.

The clearest instance of religious megalomania is the prophet. No doubt part of the reason prophets pound their chests so emphatically and roar so leoninely is to drown out the doubts in both their audience and themselves. After all, no one has ever witnessed the mysterious text-messaging from the deity that the prophets are so proud of. But having once staked their claim to being God's interlocutors with the killer intro, "Thus saith the LORD," prophets seem to go berserk: ferocious threats, delirious promises, and power, power everywhere. Jeremiah is an instructive case. His first response to the "call" from Yahweh is terror. "Ah, LORD God, behold I cannot speak, for I am a child." But God instantly bats that objection away and gives Jeremiah his first-class portfolio. "See, I have this day set thee over the nations and over the kingdoms, to root out, and to pull down, and to destroy, and to throw down, to build, and to plant" (Jer. 1.6,10). In other words, the humble priest from Anathoth has become something like the Lord of History's plenipotentiary: When Jeremiah gives the Almighty's marching orders, things happen. Eat your heart out, Henry Kissinger.

Of course, Jeremiah's actual career didn't run so smoothly, and tradition says he was murdered by his fellow Jews after being abducted to Egypt. No matter, the genre had been established; and (with a little help from Isaiah, and Elijah and Elisha and Amos before them) the prophets ran with it. First, you have some sort of hallucinations-trances, followed by the canon-roar of oracles that tell the whole world where to get off, a string of peremptory all-or-nothing propositions. Sinners, repent! Clean up your act before it's too late! You're all doomed! Disaster's on the way! You had it coming! I told you so! A megalomaniacal God inspires a team of megalomaniaal spokesmen (women need not apply), who write their ravings down and after their death continue to inspire generations of megalomaniacal preachers, who thrill their congregations with their mighty tirades (yes, some prophets *were* splendid poets, despite their constricted range).

And the browbeaten faithful seem to like being on the receiving end of the prophetic blasts. Because they feel guilty as charged? Because they think the prophet-minister is really talking about someone else? Because they're just enjoying the booming sweep of it all, the go-for-broke pyrotechnics? As Jeremiah proceeds to cry out, " From the least of them even unto the greatest of them, every one is given to covetousness, and from the prophet [i.e., his competition] even unto the priest every one dealeth falsely" (Jer. 6.13). Every single one of the bastards! How impressive is *that*? Or how about the delicious insider-sadism of Amos 3.1-3: "Hear this word that the LORD hath spoken against you, O children of Israel, against the whole family which I have brought up from the land of Egypt, saying, 'You only have I known of all the families of the earth: therefore I will punish you for all your iniquities'." Love that *therefore:* When Daddy gets home, you don't want to *know* what he's going to do to you.

Whatever the congregation's take on it, the whole prophetic show, like a late summer electric storm in the Arizona desert, generates a tremendous amount of power, which all the spectators are free to enjoy from the safety of their lightning-rodded conventicle. Never mind all the supersized fallacies saturating the atmosphere like ozone: that God exists, that he's established an infallible list of crimes and misdemeanors (the worst of which is lusting after false gods), that a mysterious corporate entity called "the people" is 100% guilty as charged of violating God's sacred rules (see "Sodom and Gomorrah, nuking of"), that overwhelming, ineluctable retaliation is just around the corner, or—weirdest of all, perhaps—that all this is as relevant as ever millennia after the prophet climbed down from his pillar and disappeared into the dust. The main thing is, the whole routine seethes with scary energy. And WE're at the center of it.

But delirium passes (as Joyce wrote in *Dubliners*). Ethics is far more complex, sermons have to be preceded by analyses and backed up by solutions. And the Wizard of Oz, aka Yahweh, Elohim, Allah, is of no use at all in this. What *would* be useful is to prick the distended balloon of His Massiveness and expose it for what it is: the bombast of the God-talkers, theomaniacal phantasmagoria. The ensuing loud pop might cause some alarm, but it would really clear our ears.

Chapter Fourteen

God Abuses Animals

> And ye shall keep it [the Passover lamb or goat] up until the fourteenth day of the same month: and the whole assembly of the congregation of Israel shall kill it in the evening. And they shall take of the blood, and strike it on the two side posts and on the upper doorpost of the houses, wherein they shall eat it. And they shall eat the flesh in that night, roast with fire . . . Eat not of Iitraw, nor sodden at all with water, but toast with fire; his head with his legs, and with the purtenance thereof.
>
> —Exodus 12.6-9

> Doth God take care for oxen?
>
> —1 Corinthians 9.8

Well, that one was a no-brainer for St. Paul—and most of theistic tradition. Of course not. Nor could Jews or Christians quarrel with the Qur'an when it says (6:142), "Of the beasts you have, some are for carrying burdens, some for slaughter." But the massive record of the LORD's indifference to the animal kingdom and still "lower" forms of life and matter isn't just one more strike against a batter already prone to whiffing; it's a piece of corroborative evidence in the case for God as a human projection. We keep denigrating animals ("beastly" vs. "humane" behavior, etc.), so why not assume that the Almighty shares and exceeds our *de haut en bas* arrogance? And assume is what the God-talkers did and do.

It's a familiar story. Yahweh in Genesis 2.19 has all the beasts of the field and the fowls of the air queue up in front of Adam to see what name—i.e., identity—he'll give them. This after he has bidden the first human (and his successors) "have dominion" (literally, stomp all over, *kivshuah*) the earth; since humans are not just the "stewards" of creation, as Christian environmentalists like to say, but in a real sense its gods. "Yet you have made them (i.e., us) little less than God; and crowned them with glory and honor. You have given them dominion over the works of your hands; you have put all things under their feet" (Psalm 8. 5-6). (See Chapter Thirteen, "Divine Megalomania: It's Catching.")

And that's pretty much how it goes for the rest of the Bible (and the Qur'an). Animals are here for our use, to be exploited or killed and eaten (except the *tref* ones). Domesticated (=enslaved) beasts get a day off on the Sabbath; but that's just a happy accident since their owners are more or less home-bound then and can't very well order the livestock to go out and plow or pull all by themselves. The intrinsic brutality and cruelty of all God-approved butchery finds vehement expression in I.B. Singer's story, "The Slaughterer," whose protagonist Yonah Meir is driven to lunacy and suicide by the realization that, as a protester against cruelty to animals, he is more compassionate than God. In another story, "The Letter Writer," Singer's alter ego Herman Gombiner reflects: "In relation to them all [animals], all people are the Nazis; for the animals it is an eternal Treblinka." That was the sort of remark that got Singer into trouble with Jews, and not just the Orthodox.

Other cultures may have venerated or even worshiped animals, but not the Jews or Christians or Muslims. When Ezekiel has his vision of dreadful goings-on in the temple of Jerusalem, one of the worst is the depiction of beasts on its walls: "So I went in and saw; and behold every form of creeping things, and abominable beasts, and all the idols of the house of Israel" 8.10). Talk about disgusting . . .

Maybe the fault lies with the animals, who are notoriously uninterested in God. Walt Whitman said in *Song of Myself* [32]:

> I think I could turn and live with animals, they are so placid and selfcontain'd,
> . . . They do not sweat and whine about their condition,
> They do not lie awake in the dark and weep for their sins,
> They do not make me sick discussing their duty to God,
> Not one is dissatisfied, not one is demented with the mania of owning things,
> Not one kneels to another, nor to his kind that lived thousands of years ago,
> Not one is respectable or unhappy over the whole earth.

Such indifference is understandable, given the fact that no animals whatsoever are invited to the afterlife, with the dubious folkloric exceptions of Leviathan and the Wild Ox, who will get butchered and eaten as entrees at the Grand Eschatological Banquet.

But there are many other reasons why God and the beasts (including the *animalia rationalia*) don't work well together. Think about it: Animals are entirely encompassed by their bodies; God is disembodied. Animals live in their senses; God apparently has no sense organs—he must lead a very dull life, minus physical vision, hearing, taste, touch, and smell. (See Chapter Seven, "God is a Spirit—But What's That?"). Animals, who have been programmed by natural selection, do whatever they have to do. God is by definition absolutely free and autonomous (but he never does or wants to do evil, stupid, or impossible things—he has to play by his own rules). Animals are entirely submerged in time: their lives are brief and fading; they are constantly moving and changing; and they perish, not just individually but as species (the vast majority of all species that have ever existed are now extinct).

Whereas God . . . the voice trembles, the mind boggles: God is beyond time and space, he generates eternity; he always was and always will be. As he tells the prophet Malachi (3.6), "I am the LORD; I change not." Animals, and all living things, are members of a species, a genus, a family, an order, a class, a phylum, a kingdom, and a domain; while God is utterly—one might almost say appallingly—unique (which may be why Christian theologians thought up the Trinity: to give God some kind of love life).

All animals are at least occasionally social, but God is so beyond any relation of dependence and need that philosophers have at times been hard-pressed to link him to terrestrial reality. Since the universe wasn't created until a certain point in time (as it were), he must have spent a practically infinite period all by himself. Why, then, did he break the silence with his "Let there be light"? It couldn't have been because he wanted company or amusement, because that would imply a lack and hence an imperfection. So, he must have called the universe into existence *ex nihilo* from sheer generosity or playfulness or rainy-day boredom or, some have even argued, love for his creatures, though he often gives them rather miserable lives.

Putting aside the perpetual carping questions about God's failures in not making the world a more pleasant home for its inhabitants, we still have to wonder why he should especially care about the earth—what's in it for him? His connection to his creatures can't be one of love as we know it, since love always means need and vulnerability; and God is invulnerable. Even if God merely loved us as his prattling pets (though how could be keep track of us all?), we know how attached we can get to cats and dogs, and how much distress their suffering causes us—but, once again, that model can't apply to le bon Dieu, der liebe Gott. He can't feel grief or even worry.

Actually, at one brief point in the Bible we get an insight that might have transformed the whole sorry tale of monotheism vs. the animals. In Ecclesiastes 3.18-21 we find the dark reflection: "I said in my heart concerning the sons of men, that God might manifest them, and that they themselves might see that they themselves are beasts. For that which befalleth the sons of men befalleth beasts; even one thing befalleth them: as the one dieth, so dieth the other; yea, they have all one breath, so that a man hath no pre-eminence above a beast: for all is vanity. All go unto one place, all are of the dust, and all turn to dust again. Who knoweth the spirit of man that goeth upward, and the spirit of the beast that goeth downward to the earth?" You won't hear *that* in church any time soon.

But the Epicurean reflections of whoever wrote Qoheleth (which only made it into the canon because of its false attribution to King Solomon) have never carried much weight with orthodox Jews and Christians. The radical idea that humans and animals are essentially alike—as seen in the fact that they die forever, when their "spirit" (breath of life) disappears—might have prompted a reappraisal of the more or less monolithic speciesism one sees in Scripture. (To be sure, Ecclesiastes himself wasn't pleading for kindness to animals; his point is that *we* are nothing much. On that issue, a later Epicurean, Michel de Montaigne, was far more enlightened; cf. his *Apology for Raymond Sebond*, which revels in the amazing talents of animals.)

But, of course, that sort of reappraisal never came. Almost a millennium later we have Muhammad advocating the same old divinely justified view of animals. Although he waxes indignant (e.g., in 7:76) over the slaughter of the she-camel Allah sent as a sign to the people of Thamud, that's the exception that proves the rule: "We have made camels a part of God's rite. They are of much use to you. Pronounce over them the name of God as you draw them up in line and slaughter them; and when they have fallen to the ground eat of their flesh and feed the uncomplaining beggar and the demanding suppliant. Thus have we subjected them to your service, so that you may give thanks" (2:36). The camels' response to this sacred dispensation has not been recorded.

In all fairness it must be said that the Catholic Church—the most pagan and least "pure" monotheistic religion—has a corps of animal-loving saints: Jerome and the lion, Giles and the deer, Francis of Assisi and the wolf of Gubbio, Anthony of Padua preaching to the fishes, etc. (And Anglican Kit Smart was entranced by his cat Jeoffrey.) But such warm-hearted, naïve theriophily doesn't extend to the Lord of Hosts. He has other things on his mind—so the prophets tell us—and just doesn't care about animals except (to some extent) the human kind..

So, the sensible thing to do would be to return the favor and ignore him the way our brother and sister beasts do (once we've got the God-killing and burying and obituary-writing phase out of the way). After all, we have nothing in common with him. He can't know, not existentially anyway, what it's like to be human (we ourselves have only the faintest glimmering of how the world appears to the animals who share most of our DNA). He knows everything in advance and from all eternity, so he never gets surprised or excited. Our lives are more like the lives of bugs and slugs than they are like his. He was so recklessly contemptuous of animals ("natural brute beasts, made to be taken and destroyed," says 2 Peter 2.12) that he had no qualms about drowning every single creature on earth for the selfish thrill of punishing the human race—which was only in its tenth generation at the time of the Flood, a pitifully small group in comparison with the vast populations of mammals, birds, and reptiles he must have whacked along with the people. What a jerk.

On the other hand, we might develop a new respect for the benighted idolaters, endlessly savaged in the Bible ("Their molten images are wind and confusion," Isaiah 41.29). All images of God are *strengst verboten*, of course; still more, any images of divinized animals, from bull calves on down—but why? All non-human animals strike us as more less uncanny and wonderful. (Even the Bible, in Proverbs 30.19, marvels at the way snakes crawl and eagles fly.) Worshiping them is a little naïve, but at least it stays within the realm of nature instead of straying out into the etherial emptiness of theology. Animals, bless them, are real. God is not.

Chapter Fifteen

God is So Sexy

> And when I [God] passed by you [Jerusalem], and saw you weltering in your blood, I said to you in your blood, "Live, and grow up like a plant of the field." And you grew up and became tall and arrived at full maidenhood; your breasts were formed, and your hair had grown; yet you were naked and bare.
>
> And when I passed by you again and looked upon you, behold you were at the age for love, and I spread my skirt over you, and covered your nakedness; yea, I plighted my troth to you and entered into a covenant with you, says the LORD God, and you became mine.
>
> —Ezekiel 16.6-8

> Divorce me, untie or break that knot again;
> Take me to you, imprison me, for I,
> Except you enthrall me, never shall be free,
> Nor ever chaste, except you ravish me.
>
> —John Donne, *Holy Sonnets*, 14

God, we are told by religious experts, has no sex "himself," but he knows all about it. He's beyond gender, but he seems to fret over it all the time (whence his long list of sex-related instructions and prohibitions in the Torah, canon law, and sharia). His names (Elohim, theos, Deus, etc.) are all masculine; and he's conventionally given masculine personal pronouns and adjectives, at least in part because the use of the feminine forms would suggest weakness and subordination—or something. He's a mighty male ruler, a fierce warrior, and an avenging judge. Alone of all the major theistic clubs, the Roman Catholic and Eastern Orthodox Churches have tried to bring some femininity into the picture, with their highly unbiblical cult of Mary, the Mediatrix of all graces and and co-Redemptrix. (But, for the record, she's also the ultimate male-identified woman—the obedient daughter, humble handmaid, surprise-spouse, and submissive mother of God.) Male mystics and pious poets, like John of the Cross and John Donne, sometimes feminize themselves vis-à-vis God (imagine a writer who'd dare to speak of ravishing God); and that's in effect what all believers do, without the overtly gender-bending language (blush). In contemporary America, apart from his un-wavering support for traditional marriage, God is thought to hold very strong opinions on homosexuality and abortion (see the "Goddoggerel" that concludes this chapter). He's a clergyman's man.

The most prolonged metaphorical treatment of God's sexuality can be found in the Hebrew prophets, who weave endless variations on Is-rael-as-adulterous/whorish-wife and Yahweh-as-furious-husband. Their logic is pellucid: the covenant between God and his people resembles a marriage, an intimate, but unequal relationship (the two biblical words for "husband," the Hebrew *ba'al* and the Greek *kyrios*, also mean "mas-ter" or "owner"). Flawless as he is, God never strays (whom would he stray with?); but his "wife," alas, often runs after third-rate pagan gods, who feeble as they are, can still arouse his jealousy. Isaiah jumps right into it in Chapter 1: "How is the faithful city become a harlot!" (v. 21). Jeremiah continually rails away, "Hast thou seen that which backsliding Israel has done? She is gone up upon every high mountain and under every green tree [the site of pagan nature cults], and there hath played the harlot" 3.6). But the keenest celebrator of this theme is Ezekiel who filled two chapters, 16 and 23, with the most lurid writing in the Bible.

E.g., "And the Babylonians came to her [Jerusalem, the southern kingdom] into the bed of love, and they defiled her with their lust; and after she was polluted by them, she turned from them in disgust. When she carried on her harlotry so openly and flaunted her nakedness, I turned in disgust from her, as I had turned from her sister [Samaria, the north-ern kingdom]. Yet she increased her harlotry, remembering the days of her youth, when she played the harlot in the land of Egypt and doted upon her paramours there, whose members were like those of asses, and whose issue was like that of horses. Thus you longed for the lewdness of your youth, when the Egyptians handled your bosom and pressed your young breasts." (RSV, 23.17-21). Down, boy!

The general drift is clear: Yahweh is king of the patriarchal order, to which women, with their wavering loyalties and tetchy rebelliousness, pose a constant threat. In fact, it's the oldest joke in the book: Just like the vexed human males he stands in for, the LORD can't live with the "virgin daughter of Israel" and can't live without her. (Christians maintain that God got so disgusted with her behavior that he filed for divorce and transferred his affections from the Synagogue to the Church). So, all the theistic religions (along with most of the others as well) insist on putting and keeping women in their place—and no one can deny that they've done a bang-up job of it. Male domination of the theistic world is so well-nigh complete, one might wonder whether men weren't driven to fashion the whole thing out of that pandemic, but seldom recognized, psychic disease, uterus-envy: Since they couldn't match women's breathtaking capacity for creating life, they invented a supreme male Life-Giver by way of compensation—and excluded women from all important dealings with him.

Islam in particular (see Chapter Sixteen, "The Death of Allah: Another God Bites the Dust"), has striven mightily to keep women down, whereas with the fading of literal faith in Judaism and Christianity a certain amount of pro forma liberation has crept in there. The one area in America, if not the West as a whole, where the androcentric God still throws his weight around (apart from homosexuality) is abortion. Biblical homophobia (aimed almost entirely against gays, not lesbians) seems to have its roots in Israel's age-old obsession with progeny (homosexual women wound up getting "given in marriage" and impregnated willy-nilly, so their sexual preferences didn't matter). But the anti-abortion craze, with God the Father as the founder, defender, and avenger of natalism, is a modern invention. There's no sacred text to back it up (the fetus simply wasn't considerted a person in the Law); and the whole obsession could actually be refuted on theological grounds—if the theomaniacs ever bothered to think consistently. Whence the following jingle, preceded by the indispensable theological and Scriptural epigraphs:

Yahweh Greets the Zygotes

In virtue of the one eternal act of the Will of the Creator, Who is of course ever present at every portion of His creation, the soul of every new human being begins to exist when the cell which generation has provided is ready to receive it as its principle of life.

—"Abortion," *The Catholic Encyclopedia* (1907)

And I thought the dead, who have already died, more fortunate that the living, who are still alive; but better than both is the one who has not yet been, and has not seen the evil deeds that are done under the sun.

—Ecclesiastes 4.2-3

As mad pro-lifers march in rows,
And fetophiliacs propose
To tear up Row v. Wade (and more:
Arrest M.D.s! Padlock the door
To all abortion clinics!) How?
Amend the Constitution—now!
(Forget that rape-or-incest clause,
A curse on baby-killing laws!)

As priests and pols (a canting crew)
Stir up this theo-bio brew,
As "silent screams" and taped-shut lips,
Proclaim some grim apocalypse,
As right-to-lifers pose and prate,
Pretending to adjudicate
Where only God can call the shots,
The Lord is busy doing lots
More crucial stuff: He must decide
The fate of tiny souls that died
Before they ever could be born,
The soulkins prematurely shorn
Of life, all those untimely ripped
From wombs or else just not equipped
To live outside. In any case,
These nano-humans have to face
Almighty God on his great throne,
To learn if they're to gloat or groan

God is So Sexy

In everlasting weal or woe—
It's called the Yahweh Judgment Show.

And here, in fact, is how He greets
(While angels show them to their seats)
The new arrivals (ranged by size):
"Well, how ya doin', little guys?
Relax! You're not on trial, no way!
You're home free, kids; you're here to stay.
Your record's clean, a spotless blank
I'll never chide you, never spank.
You've got no 'merits'? What the hell,
You likely would've done real well.
Too bad you never got the chance.
That's not your fault, just happenstance.
No dousing with baptismal water?
No problem! I'm the star Aborter.
You heard that right: The reason why
The bulk of you were forced to die
Is shoddily built uteri
Or other engineering flaws
(All my mistake!) that often cause
Poor zygotes to get flushed away,
Aborted, killed, you might well say,
By my Intelligent Design
(or not-so-smart designing—fine.
I do the best I can), so let's
Just let the past be past. Regrets?

"Forget it, team. I'll tell you what:
You may not want to hear this; but
It's God's own truth: That life you missed?
Cut off by some abortionist,
(Divine or human, all the same)?
That hearts-a-pounding, thrilling game
Of life you never played? The sight
Of extra-uterine 'delight'?
It sucks! (Forgive the vulgar phrase.
But life on earth's a vulgar craze.)
You lucky ducks, your lot's sublime:
You bailed right out of space and time.
You skipped the worst, you snagged the best;
By any standard, you are . . . blest.

"Don't take my word on this grand theme.
Ask Solomon, wise man supreme.
He'll tell you: 'Listen, embryos,
And fetuses (our world's no-shows),
Don't buy it. Life is vanity
Futility, insanity,
Absurdity, inanity.'
And one more thing, now Sol, poor guy,
Thought life was over once you die,
Whereas my Christian children, who
Know so much better, still pursue
Their wild campaign to banish choice
And drown out every other voice.

"Truth is, their 'faith' is mostly fake:
They talk of heaven, but don't take
It seriously. Else why prevent
Those fledgling souls from being sent
To *guaranteed* eternal bliss
(My grace can't fail!): each little miss
And mister, safe from sin and hell,
Far happier than tongue can tell.
And so when next you chance to meet
A rabid Christian on the street,
Be sure to tell the zygote-lover
Just this (then quickly run for cover):
'Be logical, you bloody sod:
Abortion is the path to God.'"

Naturally, this little exercise in Christian natalist logic would never convince any true-believer, for a variety of reasons, including the little-discussed fact that Christians as a group aren't really too confident about the existence of the afterlife. For one thing, they exert themselves just as feverishly as unbelievers to avoid landing there any earlier than they have to—maybe more feverishly than unbelievers, out of residual terror at the possibility of hell. Rather than die a martyr to the Jewish assassins who threatened him, Paul appealed to Caesar, in hopes of living on for a few more years. In his Letter to the Philippians, he adds: "I am in a strait betwixt two, having a desire to depart, and be with Christ, which is far better; nevertheless to abide in the flesh is more needful for you. And having this confidence I know that I shall abide" (1.23-25). So, heaving a sigh, he decided to go on living.

Given such weakness on the part on the ultimate theological bruiser, it's no wonder that ordinary anti-abortionist church ladies and lads take so little comfort in the thought of zygotes being wafted through the Pearly Gates. They can imagine (or so they pretend) a dead body, i.e., the soul that once inhabited it, escaping extinction. But a dead fetus, understandably, seems about as kaputt as you can get (quite apart from the problem bedeviling some lunatic literalists'of whether *unbaptized* dead fetuses could ever be admitted into the divine presence).

But, soteriological niceties aside, why should the Celestial Gas-Bag care in the least about abortion or any other short-term ob-gyn issue? He's the absolute Master of life and death, we're told; so surely in the long run he'll manage everything to his sublime, specifications, won't he? Then again, why should he care any more about our sexual and reproductive lives than we do about whatever it is the billions of dust mites in our houses do in that department? (Or have theologians pulled a fast one by exaggerating the distance separating us minuscule creatures from The Almighty?) The bottom line in all God-talk is always the same: Some silly men have said all sorts of silly things about their Imaginary Friend (and Enemy), then have quick-frozen these interesting projections into dogma, for the delight and torment of succeeding generations of deluded ninnies. Of course, that's no reason for other people, once they're undeluded, to pay much attention to all that nonsense.

Chapter Sixteen

The Death of Allah: A Consummation Devoutly to be Wished

> And all those nations! We destroyed them for the wrongs they did, and for their destruction We set a predestined time.
> —(Qur'an 18:59)

> How many cities, teeming with sin, have We laid waste! They lie in desolate ruin, their wells abandoned and their proud palaces empty. (22:45)

> How many nations have We destroyed who once flourished in wanton ease! The dwellings they left behind are but scarcely inhabited; We ourself were the only heirs. (28:58)

As everyone in Academe knows, criticism of Islam is off limits nowadays. Part of this ban is due, ironically, to the ascendancy of the late Professor Edward Said (a dogged secularist who hated Islam) and his error-strewn screed, *Orientalism*, whose popularity has survived its author's death. Everything westerners say about Islamic culture(s) has been declared inauthentic, hegemonic, and hopelessly poisoned by the legacy of colonialism. I once experienced this taboo first-hand when I attended a lecture by an imam from Albany, NY, whom I queried about the repulsive Qur'anic ukase in 4:33: "As for those (women) from whom you fear disobedience, admonish them, forsake them in beds apart, and beat them." (Readers with time on their hands might want to google "wife-beating in Islam" to scan the current debate swirling around this verse.) Rather than address my question, the imam started screaming that I had no right to discuss the issue since I didn't know any Arabic. Well, he was right. I don't know any Arabic; but to my decadent occidental brain *everything* is fair game to honest criticism, and that's what I hope to provide here.

The Qur'an is a storehouse of reasons for rejoicing over the death of God. No doubt the phantasm of Allah living on in the brains of a billion-plus Muslims is a much more agreeable figure than the ogre enshrined in the pages of the Qur'an. And liberal-minded Muslims (is there a web site or phone number for contacting such folks? The cogent critic of Islam known as Ibn Warraq is a professor at an undisclosed college in Ohio, where he goes without that life-saving *nom de guerre*) would likely protest against the seizing on and making too much of Muhammad's often unfortunate-to-horrible language. But the Qur'an calls itself God's eternal word (and large minority of the world's population believe this loopy claim), so it seems fair to borrow a line from the nobleman to the wicked servant in Luke 19.22: "Out of thine own mouth will I judge thee."

The first suspicious feature about Allah (or Muhammad, the two continuously blend together, as do all theists and their creations) is his insecurity. The very first verse in the Qur'an after the Exordium is, "This Book is not to be doubted" (2:1). From then on Allah-Muhammad can't stop praising his own handiwork. In 12:1, 26.1, 43:1, and 50.1, the Qur'an lauds itself as "the Glorious Book." In 16:89 it calls itself "a Book which manifests the truth about all things [*all* things?], a guide, a blessing, and good news to those who submit." Speaking of which, there's some good news/bad news puffery in 17.82, where Allah-Muhammad calls the revelations in the Qur'an "a balm and a blessing to the believers, although it only adds to the wrongdoers' prospects of damnation" (including, no doubt, the present writer's). Shortly afterwards in 17:89, which expands on a boast in 2:23, we learn that the Qur'an is incomparably great: "If men and jinn combined to produce a book akin to this Koran, they would surely fail to produce its like, though they helped one another as best they could." That's no surprise, since the Qur'an "could not have been devised by any but God . . . It is beyond doubt from the Lord of the Universe" (10:37). Of course, no writer alive need fear the literary efforts of those non-existent jinn.

Still, you'd think the All-Wise One might have been better organized, not to mention less sexist, homophobic, and vindictive; but there can be no doubt that God himself is the actual author: "This Koran could not have been devised by any but God" (10:37). "A Book, whose verses are perfected and then made plain, from Him who is wise and all-knowing" (11:1). It's like those CNN announcers who repeatedly intone their mantra about having "the best political team in television": Shut up, one wants to say in both cases, *we*'ll decide about that.

Not convinced yet of the Qur'an's splendiferousness? "This is eloquent Arabic speech" (16:103, ditto in 36.70). Not only is it "in the Arabic tongue" (imagine that!), but the Qur'an is "free from any flaw" (39:28)—so long as you don't count bitter personal outbursts, ranting, repetitiousness, incoherence, and non-stop divine fee-fi-fo-fum as flaws. The Qur'an, readers may be disappointed to hear, "is a transcript of the eternal Book in Our [Allah's] keeping, sublime and full of wisdom" (43:2). Um, you mean this is as good as it gets? Afraid so, kaffirs. As the eminent German scholar Theodor Nöldeke (d. 1930), quoted by Ibn Warraq, says: "[Muhammad], in short, is not in any sense a master of style." But then he was only taking dictation through the medium of Gabriel; so the anacolutha, awkward syntax, narrative clumsiness, and the like have to be laid at the feet of—gulp—God himself.

Well, of course, Allah never existed to begin with, except as a figment of Muhammad's overheated imagination (born as the illiterate merchant was going through a male mid-life crisis). And if Muhammad hadn't met with such resistance from the pagan Meccans, as well as from Jews and Christians, he undoubtedly would have taken a far less bonkers tone in preaching his message. But if nothing else, the Qur'an keeps reminding us what a terrible idea God was to begin with, and how wise we were to jettison him. The God of the Bible is certainly a noxious creature, but his evil traits sometimes get obscured by the vivid narratives in which he appears. Unfortunately, Allah builds on his elder brother's worst habits (and, as the Qur'an's garbled version of the adventures of Joseph in surah 12 shows, Muhammad never learned how to tell a story.)

First of all, there's the old obsession with idolatry, which, we're told (2:192), is more odious than bloodshed. Since idolatry is the worst possible human crime, it's no surprise that idolaters get lumped together with evildoers, as if a kind and gentle idolater were a contradiction in terms. Unbelievers are likewise equated with evildoers, presumably because anyone who has heard Muhammad's message but not accepted it must be morally deaf, dumb, and blind—even as the penalty for converting to any religion *from* Islam is (to this day, where practicable) death.

From the very beginning (2:5) Muhammad informs us that the infidels' "sight is dimmed and grievous punishment awaits them." What a monster, always huffing and puffing and threatening to send people to hell (mentioned over a hundred times in the Qur'an, which puts the New Testament to shame in that regard).

Allah does speak up from time to time about social and ethical issues. He encourages philanthropy, war, and polygyny, especially for Muhammad. He attacks male homosexuality (26:166, 29:28—like Yahweh, he doesn't seem to have heard about lesbianism); but he has no quarrel with slavery (33:5) or child marriage (65:4). Bernard Lewis reports that as 19th century anti-slavery movements began to spill over into Islamic countries, the stiffest resistance to abolition came from Mecca and Medina: "The emergence of the holy men and the holy places as the last-ditch defenders of slavery against reform is only an apparent paradox. They were upholding an institution sanctified by scripture, law, and tradition" (*Race and Slavery in the Middle East*, pp. 78-79).

On the whole, Allah seems to be mostly concerned with himself—whether he's getting the full measure of trembling respect and so forth. Though he gives his divine support to Muhammad's doings, he puts all this-worldly affairs into perspective by repeating that, "The life of this world is but a sport and a diversion. It is the life to come that is the true life" (29:64). Allah's Big Apocalyptic Production is what matters most. But not until Doomsday will Allah unleash the cataclysmic, annihilating forces that he's made only selective use of so far (see the three epigraphs to this chapter—Sodom and Gomorrah and all that jazz). Till then he only growls from behind a cloud.

So where does this leave us? First of all, who is Allah anyway? Ecumenical spirits like to conflate Allah with Elohim (or El) and translate both names simply as "God." If Allah and the God of the Bible are the same person (until Yahweh goes trinitarian), we could try them both together in the supreme court of reason, with an inevitable sentence of death by contempt. The major problem here is political: Yahweh is more or less defined as the God of Israel (or, as many Muslims would say, the Zionist entity). This, given the ongoing troubles in Gaza and the West Bank, makes it unlikely that the two Gods—if they were real—would ever agree to make a joint appearance, much less merge, as Daimler and Chrysler tried doing for a while. And then the Jews created all sorts of problems by refusing to accept Islam, even as they turned a deaf ear to the Gospel—and were rewarded by being nastily smeared in the sacred

Revelations of both Christians and Muslims, not to mention persecuted and murdered for centuries.

On the whole, it seems best to treat Allah as a sort of God-with-attitude. That is, although Muhammad plainly got many ideas about Allah from talking to Jews and Christians (even if ill-educated Muslim fundamentalists keep denying this), the Qur'an suffers from a defect akin to that of the New Testament vis-à-vis the Old: it's too narrow in scope Even if it wasn't composed, as devout Muslims believe, by a single author over a twenty-or-so year period, it lacks the grand choral span of the Hebrew Bible, with its host of authors (or inspired stenographers) and sources stretching over something like a millennium, and its rich mix of conflicting tones and viewpoints. And, as opposed to the various evolving divine figures in the Bible, the Qur'an gives us a monotonous haranguing Allah-one-note who deserves to be singled out for scorn both because he echoes so many bad features of Yahweh's voice and because he continues to find so many gullible listeners.

Of course, in the Jewish year of 5769, the year of Our Lord 2009, or anno Hegirae 1431, it's still essentially verboten to criticize the deity—except within the secure confines of a book printed and read in a non-Muslim country. *De mortuis nil nisi bonum.* In the final analysis, the erasure of God/Allah from the consciousness of the masses—assuming the world isn't destroyed first—will be achieved not by polemics but by a swelling tide of indifference. Still, in the very long meantime before that happens—if it ever does—why not pay a tribute to truth by repeating what should be, but isn't, obvious (not to the vast genuflecting or bowing majority anyhow) that God in general and Allah in particular is dead and richly deserves his death?

Doubters are advised to simply read the Qur'an. They can ignore, if they wish, Allah's odious misogyny ("Women are your fields; go, then, into your fields whence you please" [2:223], his infantile magical thinking ("He that hates you [Muhammad] shall remain childless" [108:3], or his psychotic animus against non-Muslims ("When you meet the unbelievers in the battlefield strike off their heads" [47:4].) But there really ought to be a limit to how much fire-breathing theistic rodomontade we have to endure. Deities who not only wipe out whole cities and nations, but who repeatedly boast about it, have outlived any usefulness they may have had. (See the epigraphs to this chapter.) Since, like HAL in *2001: A Space Odyssey*, Allah can't be reasoned with or won over to less destructive ways, he'll just have to be disconnected.

Meanwhile, millions, no tens, hundreds of millions of Muslims continue to prostrate themselves in slavish submission to an uncanny force they have never seen, heard, touched, tasted, or smelled, but have nonetheless been trained to adore. (Since Islam means "submission," it's curious that no one has connected those mass prostrations to their obvious parallels in the animal world, e.g., the submissive display of dogs or wolves before an alpha-male. Like their canine counterparts, Muslims adopt the potentially life-saving posture of abject, scrunched-together helplessness before the cosmic Mighty Dog, the better to arouse his trademark compassion.) Naturally, Allah doesn't *need* this pathetic orgy of bowing and scraping; and, if he had any taste, he'd be embarrassed by it. But he plainly thinks that worship, apart from being his legal right, is good for his admirers. It reminds the uppity little buggers just where they fit into the grand godly scheme of things—face down on the ground. If it seems strange that such a huge portion of humanity could be so thoroughly deluded, recall that the great majority of the human race likewise continues to brutalize, slaughter, and devour animals, often with the blessing of their imagined deity and after having sacrificed the poor creatures in his honor (as in Eid-ul-Adhaa).

Some squeamish humans may shrink from bloody flesh, but God has always had a hankering for it, ever since Noah's post-diluvian hecatomb of kosher beasts and fowls, when "the LORD smelled a sweet savor" (Genesis 8.21). The destruction of the Temple in 70 CE, alas, put an end to Yahweh's slaughterhouse; but Allah still gets his share of sacred butchery. And in fact he has let it be known that "the sacrificial offerings with all their ornaments" are nothing less than "eternal values for mankind" (5:97).Take *that*, wimpy Muslim vegetarians. On the other hand, why not lump together the carnivores with the theomores (God-fools)? They're equally thoughtless—and mostly dishonest. (Carnivores pretend that their neatly plastic-packaged chunks of animal protein didn't come from tortured animals; believers pretend they've actually met and somehow "know" the Great Gaseous Entity they keep talking about.) The hell with them. As the irrepressible, sometimes clownish, and but often accurate atheist Christopher Hitchens has said, God is *not* great. Least of all his latest, most popular and politically successful embodiment, the not-all-that Compassionate ("Taste now the torment of the Conflagration," 3:182) and the not-especially-Merciful ("The catastrophe of the Hour of Doom shall be great indeed," 22:1) Allah, without whom the world will be a far, far better place.

Chapter Seventeen

Jews Dispense with God—and You Can Too

> Can a maid forget her ornaments, or a bride her attire? Yet my people have forgotten me days without number.
>
> —Jeremiah 2.32

> Would that they forgot me, but kept my Torah!
>
> —Ekah Rabbah, proemium (Talmud)

> 57.1% of Jews questioned said they had doubts about whether God exists. This compares with 37% of mainline Protestants, 25% of Catholics, 13.5 % of Evangelical Protestants, and 0% of black Protestants.
>
> —2006 Baylor University study
> "American Piety in the 21st Century"

People who say "I'm Jewish" may be talking about their religion, their ethnicity, or both—it's conveniently ambiguous (e.g., for Jews in Congress, most of whom lack Joe Lieberman's Orthodox fervor, but who don't necessarily want to advertise that fact when asked about religious affiliation—and woe betide the pol without one). Surveys show that Jews are far less likely than Catholics and Protestants to attend services, believe literally in the Bible, or subscribe to a formal creed. They are particularly dubious about the Beyond. "*Olam-ha-Ba* (afterlife)," writes Rabbi Joseph Telushkin in his popular *Jewish Literacy* (1981), "is rarely discussed in Jewish life, be it among Reform, Conservative or Orthodox

Jews. This is is in marked contrast to the religious traditions of the people among whom the Jews have lived." Is it ever.

In theory—and more than theory—the Jews gave theism to the world, especially the vast Christian and Muslim parts of it; so it's curious that the people who've known God the longest and best have increasingly— ever since the Enlightenment at least—been turning their back on him The problem goes at least as back to the prophets. "Thou (Israel) hast forgotten me," complains Yahweh, speaking this time through Ezekiel, "and cast me behind thy back" (23.35). That does sound like bad behavior, considering the enormous favors God has lavished on his people, starting with his perplexing selection of them from among all the nations on earth, his philoprogenitive care for their tiny tribe, his sensational, divinely engineered Exodus, his high-handed donation of the already occupied Promised Land, etc. Perhaps God went overboard with his tirades against idolatry; but a certain amount of jealous resentment on his part seems perfectly reasonable..

This pattern of negelect no doubt has a lot to do, ironically, with one of Yahweh's most awesome benefactions to Israel: the giving of the Law on Mount Sinai/Horeb. The law is a complete guide to a godlike life. ("Ye shall be holy; for I am holy," Leviticus 11.44); and just receiving it immediately raises the Israelites to a level far above the Torah-less, clueless goyim—provided, of course, that they keep it. But once you have that guide, first inscribed on tablets, then written down in black and white, why bother with God, except maybe for old times' sake? Scripture scholars have noticed that as the Bible goes on, God gradually disappears. He stops showing up in his trademark theophanies; he stops doing miracles, and he stops speaking to the prophets (the very institution of prophecy is cursed in Zechariah 13.2-6.) The Book of Esther (like the Song of Solomon) never even mentions God's name. Is God some kind of Rodney Dangerfield?

In a way, it all makes logical, inevitable sense: Like any good parent, God has instilled a sound set of values (well, semi-sound, apart from his lapses on the condition of women, slaves, and animals, etc.) in his children, who, after the usual growing pains of boy- and girlhood and the turbulent time of adolescence, have turned into adults, now able to make it on their own without help from the Old Man (who has died anyway). Instead of forever pondering and arguing about the finer points of theology, Jewish thinkers have studied and codified and changed and improved the law, e.g., Rabbi Gershom's 10th century ban on polygamy, which overturned centuries of divinely sanctioned patriarchal privilege.

It's no secret that in the 19th century once the ghetto walls began to crumble and Jews were belatedly allowed to practice law, they poured into the legal profession and made a mark in it out of all proportion to their numbers—as they continue to do today: check your local Yellow Pages. The Torah was o.k. to cut your teeth on, but now let's get down to the REAL law, the kind that actually governs the world. Secular Jews who want to deal more with ideas and less with grubby practicalities of the tax code, contracts, or corporate mergers, can always become ethicists—and many have.

In *Elementary Structures of Religious Life* (1912) Emile Durkheim, a Jewish atheist with a distinguished rabbinical pedigree, explained that, "A society has everything necessary to awaken in people's minds, simply by the action that it exerts on them, the sensation of the divine; because it is to its members what a god is to his faithful followers." So the transition from sacred to secular law was easy, because both sorts were versions of the same thing: a collection of rules designed (by humans—who else?) to create peace and order in public life—things good in themselves that need no supernatural validation. Hence Judaism is primarily about Jews, and not about God, whom, as the prophets wail, his people keep forgetting. But why shouldn't they?—he's done his job, and he's never there when you need him anyway. Time to move on.

In the US Jews are active in aggressively non-religious groups like the ACLU, Americans United for the Separation of Church and State, People for the American Way, etc. Litigation and advertising campaigns from such bodies typically help shield Jews from the incursions of wacky fundamentalist Christians, who want the Cross to overshadow the land. But they also doubtless serve to promote secularism, which is the real religion of a great many—probably the majority of—American Jews (and other card-carrying members of America's and the world's intellectual elite).

No sooner did Jews get admitted to the mainstream of modern western life than their writers and intellectuals started attacking or undermining theism. Heinrich Heine (1797-1856) cloaked his godlessness with a sort of deistic fig leaf, but his mocking bulletin about the last moments of a dying God clearly anticipates Nietzsche by half a century. Karl Marx preached an unremitting atheism, as did Sigmund Freud. Albert Einstein is widely but mistakenly thought to have been a philosophical believer, but he firmly rejected the idea of a personal God. The corpus of modern Jewish literature, from Proust to Kafka to Isaac Babel to the Singer brothers to Primo Levi to Philip Roth, is resolutely godless.

The same is true of Jewish philosophers, anthropologists, sociologists, etc. It's hard to avoid the impression that dispatching God provided at least some of the fuel for the grand creative outburst that took off with Spinoza and continues till this day, to Steven Weinberg and beyond. It's as if the sadder-but-wiser older brothers, as soon as they were given the floor, began to show their callow Christian siblings the folly of their ways. (Most Muslims, alas, seem hopelessly befogged by the old lies. But then check which group, despite being hopelessly outnumbered, has won more Nobel Prizes.)

Jews have a clear advantage over Christians when it comes to getting rid of God in that they have more cultural substitutes to fall back on than most gentiles: keeping kosher, holding Passover seders (stressing liberation, not the Liberator), fasting on Yom Kippur and Tisha B'Av, going to shul for the High Holy Days, learning Hebrew, supporting Israel, and of course socializing with other Jews. (But current American Jewish intermarriage rates of over 50% point to the doubtful future of such cultural Judaism.) The much thinner substance of Presbyterian or Methodist or even Catholic identity doesn't allow for that kind of shift, which may be one reason why Protestants continue to give lip-service to religious ideas they don't really believe in.

Along with the God of monotheism, the Jews also gave the West what we now call family values, fusing the two creatively in the sensationally successful figure of God the Father (see Chapter Ten, "God the Father—and the Perils of Permanent Puerility"). So it's only appropriate that Dr. Freud should have provided a pointed breakdown of the whole fantasy in *The Future of an Illusion* (1927): "Now as the young person grows up, he or she discovers that he or she is that he is fated to remain a child for ever, that he or she can never do without protection against alien higher powers. So people give those powers the features of a father figure; they create for themselves the gods whom they are afraid of, whom they seek to win over, and to whom they nevertheless entrust the task of protecting them. Thus, the motive of longing for a father is the same as the need for protection against the consequences of human powerlessness. And the defense against the child's helplessness defines the characteristic features of the reaction to helplessness, which the adult must acknowledge as what shapes religion We tell ourselves that, yes, it *would* be very nice, if there was a God who created the world, and a kindly Providence, a moral world order, and a life beyond the grave. But it's very striking that all this is exactly the way we are forced to wish it. And wouldn't it be still more unusual if our poor, ignorant, unfree ancestors had managed to solve all these difficult cosmic mysteries" (Part VII).

One can find instances of such Jewish tough-mindedness everywhere in modern times, from Isaiah Berlin to Lenny Bruce to Barbara Ehrenreich to Jules Feiffer to Emma Goldman to Jackie Mason to Steven Pinker to Elie Wiesel and beyond. But these days unbelief comes cheap; and any halfway intellectually self-respecting person, Jew or Gentile, is liable to be an atheist. But go back to earlier—*much* earlier—Jewish tradition, and you can find strong traces of the same spirit. For example, there is a famous episode in the Babylonian Talmud (Baba Mezi'a 59b) that recounts the discomforture of the great Rabbi Eliezer ben Hurqanos (1st-2nd century CE), a conservative sage and member of the Sanhedrin who found himself at odds with the majority on an interpretation of the Torah. Rabbi Eliezer produced a hold-the-phone series of miracles to back up his position—but he still lost out and was put under the ban:

On that day R. Eliezer brought forward every imaginable argument, but they did not accept them. Said he to them: "If the *halachah* agrees with me, let this carob-tree prove it!" Thereupon the carob-tree was torn a hundred cubits out of its place—others affirm, four hundred cubits. "No proof can be brought from a carob-tree," they retorted. Again he said to them: "'If the *halachah* agrees with me, let the stream of water prove it!" Whereupon the stream of water flowed backwards—"No proof can be brought from a stream of water," they rejoined. Again he urged: "If the *halachah* agrees with me, let the walls of the schoolhouse prove it," whereupon the walls inclined to fall. But R. Joshua rebuked them, saying: "When scholars are engaged in a halachic dispute, what have ye to interfere?" Hence they did not fall, in honour of R. Joshua, nor did they resume the upright, in honour of R. Eliezer; and they are still standing thus inclined. Again he said to them: "If the *halachah* agrees with me, let it be proved from Heaven!" Whereupon a Heavenly Voice cried out: "Why do ye dispute with R. Eliezer, seeing that in all matters the *halachah* agrees with him!" But R. Joshua arose and exclaimed: "It is not in heaven." What did he mean by this?—Said R. Jeremiah: That the Torah had already been given at Mount Sinai; we pay no attention to a Heavenly Voice, because Thou hast long since written in the Torah at Mount Sinai, after the majority must one incline. (Source: Soncino Talmud)

In other words, the hell with your pious razzmatazz, baby—we have to use our brains here. And when we can't agree, we have to act democratically and count heads. Leave God out of this. (And Whoever you are up there, be quiet. We don't need you.) The Catholic Church may have its brigades of miracle-working saints, its Marian apparitions at Lourdes, Fatima, etc., its *credo quia impossibile*'s. And Christians of all denominations may cheer for those booming celestial endorsements ("This is my beloved Son, in whom I am well pleased!" Matthew 3.17, etc.), while the Islamic umma revels in its over-the-top veneration of Muhammad (death to cartoonists!) But the Jews can get by with rational discussion and voting. And so can we. You don't have to be Jewish to love rationality.

Chapter Eighteen

A Humorless God

> And the LORD spake unto Moses and unto Aaron, saying, How long shall I bear with this evil congregation, which murmur against me? I have heard the murmurings of the children of Israel, which they murmur against me. Say unto them, As truly as I live, saith the LORD, as ye have spoken in mine ears, so will I do to you: Your carcases shall fall in this wilderness; and all that were numbered of you, according to your whole number, from twenty years old and upward, which have murmured against me, Doubtless ye shall not come into the land, concerning which I sware to make you dwell therein, save Caleb the son of Jephunneh, and Joshua the son of Nun. But your little ones, which ye said should be a prey, them will I bring in, and they shall know the land which ye have despised. But as for you, your carcases, they shall fall in this wilderness.
>
> —Numbers 14.26-32

God has no sense of humor—but who expects him to have one? The job of minding the fractious human race 24/7 might well exhaust and depress even the supremest of Beings. And since people constantly fail to do what they're told, God *has* to maintain his disciplinarian's demeanor. This can often get off-putting, as in the passage above, where God condemns the entire Exodus generation to die and leave their bones to bleach in the sands of the Sinai before their children enter Canaan.

But, bad as this is (like Yahweh's later horripilating prediction, in Deuteronomy 28, of cannibalism at the siege of Jerusalem in 586 BCE—to punish a later sinful generation—or Jesus' and Muhammad's vivid threats of hell), it's not *tragic* Technically, you can't have any tragedy where God is involved (i.e., everywhere, if we but knew), since he makes no mistakes and is 1000% just, unlike us. If everything is (ultimately) done right, what's to complain about? The Greek gods had an often brutal way of dishing out justice, where the punishment, to mortal eyes at least, greatly exceeds the crime (e.g., the agony of Pentheus and Agave in *The Bacchae*), but you can't say that about Yahweh or Allah, whose hands are always spotless . At the end of every eternal sentence signed by The Judge there might well stand a exultant bold-face QED. Any questions? I thought not.

Still worse, it seems you can't do comedy with God either. Most comedy deals in mild (or gleeful) sadism (Hobbes's "sudden glory") or physical exuberance (our happy animal self takes over), which are evidently off-limits for God. Actually, God often *sounds* as if he likes seeing humans suffer—and not just Yahweh and Allah, at times even supposedly gentle Jesus gets carried away by a rush of vengefulness: "And thou, Capernaum, which art exalted unto heaven, shalt be brought down to hell: for if the mighty works, which have been done in thee, had been done in Sodom, it would have remained until this day. But I say unto you, That it shall be more tolerable for the land of Sodom in the day of judgment, than for thee" (Matthew 11.23-24).

Perhaps this subversive reading is due to our tone-deaf secular ears. Theologians tell us that God wants only the best for us; that all we have to do is accept it—but in any case Jesus certainly isn't laughing or overtly enjoying himself in this scene. He never does. Oh, and for the record, Allah/ Muhammad is every bit as unflappably glum. ("The wrongdoers persist in error and madness. On the day when they are dragged into the Fire with faces down, We shall say to them: 'Feel the touch of Hell!'" 54:48). As one of the hadith (*Sahih al-Buikhari, vol. 8, #627)* tells us, the Prophet said, "O followers of Muhammad! By Allah, if you knew what I know, you would weep much and laugh little." Luckily, most of us *don't* know now, and never will know, what he knew.

As for exuberance, the blissful overflow of drunken or erotic energies, e.g., in Aristophanes or Rabelais, *that* plainly can't fit into the repertoire of divine feelings: God never needs relief from sensory deprivation, and he never indulges in excess. He can't be surprised (no aha- or ha-ha-moments), nor can he experience that delicious mental-labor-saving shortcut that Freud says (in *Jokes and Their Relation to the Unconscious*) makes us laugh at certain kinds of jokes. On the other hand, the tendentious (sex-and-violence) jokes that Freud thinks we savor because they give us risk-free substitute satisfactions for pleasures condemned by the law or our conscience must be equally meaningless for our unsmiling God.

Worse yet, we can't even imagine God experiencing any pleasure at all, because with us and the animals, pleasure always requires some form of prior deprivation to create the jolting contrast that creates any sensation worth writing home about. James 1.17 famously assures us that God is the "Father of lights, with whom is no variableness, neither shade of turning"; and that seems reasonable, since otherwise God would have his ups and downs, his good days and bad days, his moods and whims, etc. But then we hit the same imaginative roadblock: a constant state of pleasure (no refractory period!) isn't just unthinkable, it's impossible. And even if weren't, in the final analysis it would be a total drag (like the deity himself).

So God doesn't tell jokes. Or if he does, his special friends haven't recorded them; and those friends themselves almost never lighten up. To be fair, the Lord's concluding rhetorical question in the Book of Jonah ("Should I not spare Nineveh, that great city, wherein are more than sixscore thousand persons that cannot discern between their right hand, and their left hand, and also much cattle?" 4.11) does show some wit. But it still comes across as deadly earnest. Yahweh means business. Like all the comic parts in that great short story—Jonah the prophetic misfit running full speed ahead away from his sacred assignment, sleeping in the ship's hold right through the storm at sea, etc.—the Lord's indignant query makes the reader smile, but not the protagonists. In any event, if God did have an eye or a weakness for jokes, he'd have to face the bane of every comedian: the limited shelf-life and cultural reach of practically all punch lines. Timeless, universal humor seems to be a contradiction in terms. What knocked 'em dead in Mizpah or Medina might very well bomb in Manhattan.

But no problem there, because God doesn't even try to crack wise. When speaks out, he tends to be relentlessly emphatic (and negative): "I have nourished and brought up children, and they have rebelled against me. The ox knoweth his owner, and the ass his master's crib: but Israel doth not know, my people doth not consider" (Isaiah 1.2-3). God has to forswear, or at least dispense with, all the tricks of the comedic trade. He can't lie. He can't distort or wildly exaggerate for laughs. He can't be gross or obscene or blasphemous . He can't—God forbid—mock or make fun of himself. He can't clown around, wear silly outfits, or behave like one of the classical Tricksters, spreading havoc for comic effect. He can't (not logically anyhow) come out with staple comic rejoinders like "Who cares?" (*everything* matters to him), "You're kidding!" (you can't astonish, or put one over on, *him*), much less "O my God!" (taking his own name in vain, so to speak). Bummer. The best God can manage in the Bible is a snort of contempt—which doesn't quite qualify as humor: "He that sitteth in the heavens shall laugh; the LORD shall have them in derision (Psalm 2.4). There's not a lot of joviality in "I told you so," which must of necessity be God's sempiternal refrain, as he scans the human world (cf. Job 21. 22: "Shall any teach God knowledge?" etc.) He's heard it all before. Yawn.

The problem, after all, is that you can't give what you don't have: Both the crazed prophets who thought they'd heard God talk, and the dreaming theologians who thought they'd made philosophical sense of the prophets' hallucinatory babblings were (and continue to be) humorless types; and they wrapped the Lord in their very wet blankets. Not that they didn't have a point. Humor is subversive, and if they left any of that combustible, explosive material lying around, it might bring the whole temple down, so to speak. The heart of religion, according to Rudolf Otto, is the *mysterium tremendum et fascinans*, the burning bush, the pillar of the cloud, the Transfiguration, the Angel Gabriel's cry, "Recite!" But to maintain the proper spirit of tremulous awe, that mystery has to be treated with, at the very least, kid gloves and a straight face. Imagine, if you please, the recipient of any great scriptural miracle, Naaman the cleansed leper, say, or King Hezekiah, who got an extra fifteen years of life, the Virgin Mary, or back-from-the-dead Lazarus, exclaiming in amazement, "Holy shit!" Yes, Abraham does laugh when he hears that he and his postmenopausal wife are about to get pregnant— but once again that's just scorn.

Laughter deflates the high and mighty; it relativizes things. Once you've seen Mel Brooks's misadventure as Moses in the *History of the World: Part I*, where he drops and breaks the tablet inscribed with Commandments 11 through 15, you can't watch Charlton Heston presenting the Decalogue without a laugh. On the solemn topic of the death of God, Woody Allen notes: "Not only is God dead, but you can't get a plumber on the weekends." No wonder Yahweh had to ban it from his court entirely. In normal royal palaces the underlings are forever snickering and making jokes about the King—whenever he's safely offstage. By that standard, no God could ever be a hero to his own valets. And so this is one more reason why we had (have) to get rid of him: he's no fun at all.

Meanwhile, etherealized as he is (thanks to his theological ad agency), God has pretty much been placed beyond the range of comic treatment. (No point in harping on the feebleness of De Lawd in Marc Connelly's *Green Pastures* [1936] or the throwaway divine roles foisted on Hollywood veterans George Burns and Morgan Freeman). Unlike the thoroughly human gods of Greece, who could appear on stage and make fools of themselves in *The Birds* (Poseidon, Heracles) or *The Frogs* (Dionysus), Jehovah will not indulge in tomfoolery. Religion and the clergy have always been rich comic targets, from Boccaccio and Chaucer to Swift and Voltaire, Mark Twain and Bill Maher; but God has mostly gotten off the hook.

No doubt this is largely because—apart from the taboos still in place against dissing the Everlasting—most serious creative minds either have no interest in the God-question or think it's been decided long ago. And it has, but lots of people don't realize that; so perhaps it's time to inaugurate a new age of comic blasphemy: one more weapon to help prevent a rightly killed deity from becoming—God forbid—undead.

Of course, laughing at God might strike some people as unsporting; since not only can't he fight back, but his fans are too paralyzed by reverence for the conventions of God-talk to say anything remotely amusing. Once upon a time believers-in-chief could hurl anathemas, phone the secular arm, and kindle a crackling bonfire to repay insults to the godhead. Now all they have is the feeble arsenal of apologetics—not a shpritz to their name. But they do have a lot of powerful friends—and countless millions of feeble-minded adherents (e.g., the 74% of white Evangelicals who voted for John McCain in 2008); so enlightened theophobes will have to keep up their *feu d'enfer* at the gloomy, ill-defined castles of the godly.

There must be *some* theological laugh-lines, no? D'ja hear the one about the difference between hyperdulia and latria? The farblonzhete sefiros? The Mu'tazilah and the Ash'ariyya? Don't bother. Ever notice that all the really good jokes about the afterlife take place in hell; and all the (mostly lame) ones about heaven never get past the Pearly Gates and St. Peter's bar/wicket? Once safely arrived in eternity, what could there possibly be to laugh about? Reruns of salvation history? The pathetic fate of the eternally and oh-so-properly damned? (Do the devils sing "We will, we will ROCK you!" to the inmates of hell?) The mistakes in the Bible (two midwives in Exodus 1.15 for a population of ca 3,000,000! hares that chew the cud in Leviticus 11.6! Solomon's 1,000 bedmates—

what a man! Jesus' contradictory genealogies in Matthew 1 and Luke 3! Judas's double death, either hanged by his own hand (Matthew 27.5) or a smashed up in fall (Acts 1.18)! Hey, get a fact-checker!

Naah, even such tame objects of ridicule will have to be blanketed with the *de rigueur* emotions of the afterlife: tremulous gratitude, pious joy, thunderous praise. Sounds pretty sycophantic, but don't you dare say that—and wipe that smart-ass smile off your face. God is no joking matter—wait, actually that's all he is.

Chapter Nineteen

God Closes the Deal

> And he shewed me a pure river of water of life, clear as crystal, proceeding out of the throne of God and of the Lamb. In the midst of the street of it, and on either side of the river, was there the tree of life, which bare twelve manner of fruits, and yielded her fruit every month: and the leaves of the tree were for the healing of the nations. And there shall be no more curse: but the throne of God and of the Lamb shall be in it; and his servants shall serve him. And they shall see his face; and his name shall be in their foreheads. And there shall be no night there; and they need no candle, neither light of the sun; for the Lord God giveth them light: and they shall reign for ever and ever.
>
> —Revelation 22.1-5

> As for the righteous, they shall be lodged in peace together amid gardens and fountains, arrayed in rich silks and fine brocade. Even thus: and We shall wed them to dark-eyed houris. Secure against all ills, they shall call for every kind of fruit; and, having once died, they shall die no more. Your Lord will in His mercy shield them from the scourge of Hell. That will be the supreme triumph.
>
> —Qur'an 44:51-57

If you can believe what you see on TV, one of the things Americans desire most these days is closure. The term itself seems to be a legacy of the psychobabblers; and it's now used to mean any positive conclusion to any painful situation. When you can't have a full-throttle happy ending, closure is (much) better than nothing. It's typically applied to members of a grieving family whose loved one's body (lost in war, a natural disaster, a mining accident, etc.) has yet to be recovered, and still more to the parents and relatives of a victim whose killer has yet to be executed. (Watching that lethal injection do its work can be oh-so-comforting.) Even people who've never suffered such a misfortune and opponents of the death penalty can well imagine the need for putting traumatic tension to rest. As it happens, the God-talkers too have been obsessed with "closure" for centuries, if not millennia, as a brief glance into Scripture will show.

Many Jews of Jesus' day were fascinated by a scenario called The End of Days; and Jesus' own recorded words give a vivid account of it. "Immediately after the tribulation of those days shall the sun be darkened, and the moon shall not give her light, and the stars shall fall from heaven, and the powers of the heavens shall be shaken," etc. (Matthew 24.29). This ultra-dramatic Jewish theme of apocalypse, first seen in Isaiah 24-27, and then in Daniel 7-12 gets its grandest treatment in the Book of Revelation, which slams the door of history shut and describes God's (and Jesus') mopping-up operations, as all human beings (finally!) get their just deserts, and the trials of the virtuous are crowned with unending bliss. Muhammad too was obsessed with divine closure, and he often brackets "God" and "the Last day" (9:44) as the foundation of Islamic faith. Like Jews and Christians, the Prophet was fond of trumpets and promised that, "All sovereignty shall be His on the day when the trumpet is sounded" (6:73). St. Paul firmly promised (1 Corinthians 15.42), that trumpet WILL sound.

And then? Well, let'see, an Angel Falls of hallelujahs will cascade down (flattering The Boss non-stop for all eternity). And since closure often seems to carry a note of Schadenfreude with it, Catholic tradition holds that one of the major thrills of heaven will come from peering down to watch the agonies of the damned. As St. Thomas Aquinas explains in his Supplement (q. 94) to his *Summary of God-Talk* : "Nothing should be denied the blessed that helps to perfect their happiness. Now everything becomes better known by comparison with its opposite, because when opposites are placed side by side they stand forth more clearly. Hence, so that the happiness of the saints may be more delightful to them and that they may thank God more effusively for it, they are allowed to get a perfect view of the sufferings of the damned." Hey, Mildred, wouldja take a look at *that* guy!

This depressing vision of finality is interesting both for what it reveals and what it lacks. Most of all, it shows the desperation felt by a persecuted minority, who wanted revenge for the wrongs done them, and who had no place to turn to except the Hereafter—so bring it on! God-Jesus is the Big Brother who rescues his beleaguered siblings and dishes out a ferocious eternal beating to their tormentors. Right before Muhammad's description of Paradise cited above we read: "The fruit of the Zaqqûm tree [which grows only at the bottom of Hell] shall be the sinner's food. Like dregs of oil, like scalding water, it shall simmer in his belly. A voice will cry: 'Seize him and drag him into the depths of Hell. Then pour scalding water over his head, saying: taste this, illustrious and honourable man! This is the punishment which you have doubted'" (44:43-50). Talk about adding insult to injury . . .

So the righteous rejoice, the reprobate writhe; and the Show's over. Or rather, once the credits have rolled, the last magnificent freeze-frame hits the screen and stays there. (As do the audience—they can't stagger out blinking into the daylight, because in the afterlife, we have it on the best authority, there is neither sun nor moon [Rev. 21.23].) It turns out that even the happy believers have a high price to pay for their belated satisfaction: complete, perennial stasis.

Which tells us a lot about God—or the Judeo-Christian-Islamic fantasy of God at least. It seems he's an engine for some crucial kinds of earth-moving that are far beyond our derisory capacity. Unfortunately, that machine can't function in the here and now for all to see; so to experience the Afterlife it's going to take the aforementioned trumpet-blast, thunderclaps, and the fastest and most spectacular scene-shift ever into a wondrous new dimension where God at long last shows his stuff. And it's all, as they say, to die for—but then things get iffy (perhaps like that flash-in-the-pan male burlesque show, "The King's Cameleopard or the Royal Nonesuch" in *Huckleberry Finn*).

Once we're saved (everyone who reads or hears the apocalyptic texts presumably imagines himself or herself warbling in the heavenly choir, not howling with the damned), why do we need God? You'd warmly thank (Ta! Toodle-oo!) a lifeguard who pulled you from the undertow, but you wouldn't move in with him. And once we meet God and get to know him, will we just be transported to a state of blank ecstasy? The usual theological dodge when asked such questions is to quote 1 Corinthians 2.9 (parodied by Bottom in *A Midsummer Night's Dream*): "Eye hath not seen, nor ear heard, nor have entered into the heart of man, the things which God hath prepared for them that love him." Heaven is a surprise present so mysteriously wrapped you can't begin to envision what it might be like, so don't even try. Actually, the Gift of Gifts can only be one thing: God himself (at present seen through a glass, darkly). How's that for *obscurum per obscurius*?

We really can't make any sense of this. It defies Rule #1 of the universe: All things flow. Strictly speaking, the phrase "unchangeable reality" is meaningless. We've never experienced it. It applies neither to us nor to anything else (which is why an immutable God has to be the great Not-Even-Remotely-Like-Us at the other end of the cosmos). So we have to abandon the myth of Closure and God the Closer (though God, if he existed, would have to be a lot less irritating than Kyra Sedgwick). Judeo-Christian-Islamic "eternity" does not compute. Whatever lives moves, changes, and gets transformed (and so does whatever is dead, though in different ways). By contrast, an Unmoved Mover is both a contradiction in terms and a deadly dull idea.

Every living creature alters with everything that happens to it. But since God knows everything in advance, there can be no novelty in his so-called life. He knows a million years ahead of time—or so the God-talkers tell us—everything we're going to say to him; but he manages to stifle his yawns because he knows it's good for *us* to address him, plead with him, worship him, etc. (Perhaps he's like a Nobel Prize physicist moonlighting as a department store Santa.) But while this grossly asymmetrical relationship might, with a stretch, be seen as making some sense in the world we inhabit (see Chapter Eleven, "Your God's Too Big"), it it breaks down in the Beyond. Do the players cozy up with the referees after the game? Of course not; they shower and go home, to rest and get ready for the next game. Tomorrow is another day. Enough palm-waving already.

And all closure is by definition temporary. Like all forms of pleasure, it's relief from some sort of tension, to be followed by more tension and (if you're lucky) more relief. You pay those bills, and more come due. You fix the house, and it needs fixing again. You call the doctor, and before long you're making another appointment. You can complain about the cycle and shout "Stop!" (a lot of good *that* will do). Or you can wax philosophical, as Socrates did while rubbing his leg in prison after his fetters were removed on the day he drank the hemlock: "How strange, my friends, seems to be this thing that people call pleasure! How marvelously it relates to what seems to be its opposite, pain: They won't come to a person at the same time; but if you pusue the one and catch it, you're generally obliged to take the other too, as if the two were joined together in a single unit" (*Phaedo* 60 B).

The one thing you can't do is put an end to the process—short of expunging consciousness once and for all. You can cry out for closure all you want (everyone does); but the closure God supposedly offers is an illusion. It could, to be sure, make an enjoyable thought-experiment. Imagine, say, a gigantic Nurembeg-style trial for history's worst war criminals (most of whom got away), with a crack team of prosecutors and complete TV coverage, as the centerpiece of the Last Judgment. Or a Planetary Hospital where at long last an enormous team of top surgeons would repair to perfection every bit of damage ever done to the bodies of all God's creatures. Or we could have a glorious concert series with all the music Mozart, Schubert, Mendelsohn, and Bizet never lived to compose (because God didn't take better care of his youthful geniuses. And so on.

Actually, none of that is any more unrealistic than the scenarios of Isaiah 25.8 and Revelation 7.17 where God wipes away all the tears from the eyes of at least the saved portion of humanity. No more unrealistic, but every bit as preposterous. Still, all such dreams are perfectly in keeping with God's key function in modern times: to fill up our abyssal gaps in knowledge and control of the world, to glue together all the pieces that have been hopelessly scattered since at least 1621, when John Donne announced that all coherence was gone. But people don't give up easily (Donne went on ranting and pretending he'd found that glue till he died ten years later.)

In the end, closure, like God, does not exist. Death may bring closure to all brain-fueled activities; but the corpse goes on to pastures new, so to speak. In the strict philosophical sense, nothing ever absolutely begins or absolutely ends. The universe always was and always will be—in some shape or form. Easy come, easy go, though not for anxious observers of the scene like ourselves. And so we have to have a God to push the creational starter-button (amidst the primordial nothingness, even though the proverb tells us that nothing comes of nothing) and ring down the apocalyptic curtain. After that, the poets take over, like poor Peter Abelard (d. 1142), who had every reason to hope for a better postmortem deal:

> O quanta, qualia sunt illa sabbata
> quae semper celebrat superna curia.
> quae fessis requies, quae merces fortibus,
> cum erit omnia Deus in omnibus.
>
> vere Ierusalem est illa civitas,
> cuius pax iugis est, summa iucunditas,
> ubi non praevenit rem desiderium,
> nec desiderio minus est praemium.
>
> quis rex, quae curia, quale palatium,
> quae pax, quae requies, quod illud gaudium,
> huius participes exponant gloriam,
> si quantum sentiunt, possint exprimere.
>
> illic ex sabbato succedet sabbatum,
> perpes laetitia sabbatizantium,
> nec ineffabiles cessabunt iubili,
> quos decantabimus et nos et angeli.
>
> perenni Domino perpes sit gloria,
> ex quo sunt, per quem sunt, in quo sunt omnia;
> ex quo sunt, Pater est; per quem sunt, Filius;
> in quo sunt, Patris et Filii Spiritus.

(It's really quite a qood hymn, as hymns go, though best read in the original Latin, and I feel honor-bound to give a little time to the opposition): "O how many and how how splendid are the sabbaths celebrated in the court on high. What rest to the weary, what reward to the strong when God will be all in all! Truly [the heavenly] Jerusalem is that city, whose peace is supreme joyfulness on the mountain heights, where the desire does not outstrip the reality, nor the reward fall short of the desire. How great a king, a royal court, a palace, what peace, what rest, what tremendous joy—let those who take part in this glory express this, if they can express what they feel. Meantime, let us lift up our minds and seek our homeland with all our prayers, and finally return from Babylon to Jerusalem after long exile. There, with all our troubles ended, we shall sing, free from care, the songs of Zion, and your blessed people, Lord, will give endless thanks for the gifts of your grace. There one sabbath follows on another, the perpetual joy of the sabbath-keepers, nor will the ineffable jubilations, sung by us and the angels, ever fall silent.

Eternal glory to the Lord, from whom, through whom, in whom are all things: from the Father, through the Son, and in the Spirit of the Father and the Son."

But, don't hold your breath, beloved brethren. This scene only happens in books. You want closure?

Go read about it.

Conclusion

The Future of God

What our cheerfulness means.—The greatest recent event—that "God is dead," that belief in the Christian God has become unbelievable—is already beginning to cast its first shadows over Europe. At least for the few, whose eyes, whose *suspicious* eyes, are strong and sharp enough for this spectacle, a kind of sun seems to have set, a kind of old, deep confidence seems to have been turned all the way round into doubt. For them our old world must daily appear closer to evening, more mistrustful, stranger, "older." In the main, however, one has to say that this event itself is much too great, too distant, too far from most people's ability to grasp, for the mere report of it to be said to have *arrived* already; much less for the majority to know *what* has actually taken place—and all the things that must now collapse, since this belief has been undermined, because they were built on it, leaned on it, grew into it: for example, all our European morality. This long wealth and succession of demolition, destruction, downfall, and overthrow that lies before us: Who nowadays could guess enough of it to have to play the part of the teacher, preacher, and predictor of a darkening and a solar eclipse whose like has probably never been seen yet on earth? . . . Even we born puzzle-solvers, who are waiting, as it were, on the mountains, placed between today and tomorrow, and yoked into the contradiction between today and tomorrow, we firstborns and pre-emies of the coming century, who *ought* to have already glimpsed the shadows that must forthwith engulf Europe: Why is it that even we aren't really caught up in this darkening, and above all look to its approach without concern and fear for *ourselves*? Are we perhaps still too swayed by the *immediate consequences* of this event—and these immediate consequences, these consequences are for *us*, contrary to what one might expect, not at all sad and dark. Rather they are like a new, hard-to-describe sort of light, happiness, relief, cheerfulness, encouragement, dawn . . . In fact, we philosophers and "free spirits," when we get the news that the "old God is dead," feel as if irradiated by a new dawn. Our hearts overflow with thankfulness, astonishment, presentiment, expectation—at last the horizon looks free to us once more, even if it admittedly isn't bright. At last our ships can weigh anchor again, at whatever risk. The sea, *our* sea against lies open, perhaps there has never been such an "open sea" before.

—Nietzsche, *The Gay Science*, 343

Predicting the future may be the vainest of all human endeavors ("You will hear about it once it has happened," said Aeschylus); and history is strewn with the laughable wrecks of those who have tried to. Still, betting on a strong established pattern is far less foolhardy; and when it comes to God, we have a lot of evidence. For one thing, all over the world, outside the hysterical epicenters of Torah, canon law, and sharia, unbelief is becoming more acceptable and less dangerous. After all it's been a while since Thomas Aikenhead was hanged in Edinburgh for blasphemy (1697) and le Chevalier de la Barre was tortured and beheaded in Abbeville for a similar offense (1766). (Both poor wretches were only nineteen years old.)

Tolerance blooms in the garden of indifference; and, despite some recurrent spasms of religiosity, the western world has been growing increasingly bored with God—e.g., the fading of blue laws and the steady secularization of the sabbath, the emptying of Catholic churches in Europe and Catholic seminaries everywhere, the disappearance of hell from all but the stupidest pulpits, the spread of ecumenism (partly an overcoming of Freud's "narcissism of minor differences," but subconsciously at least a creeping awareness of the absurdity of all dogma), the increasing welcome accorded by mainstream denominations to liberal, secular causes like feminism, gay rights, freedom of speech, etc., and, inevitably, the irreversible triumphal march of materialistic explanations for everything.

The likely eventual upshot of all this—always assuming the world isn't destroyed first by divinely blessed forces like natalism, ecocide (hey, the Parousia is just around the corner), and holy wars—is the relegation of God to the innocuous status of Ancient Symbol (as opposed to Actual Ruler). This watered-down deism is already ubiquitous in our culture, as in expressions like "My God!" (=wow, arg, yipes, etc.),

"God knows" (= nobody knows) or "Goddamn X (= *I* can't do anything about it, and I doubt anyone can), "God forbid" (=what a horrible thought!), or "God's honest truth" (=truth), where neither speaker nor listener ever imagines God having anything to do with the situation. A diluted deity can also be seen in the shift from Theology to Religious Studies in Academe, from redemption to therapy in popular preaching (see Fareed Zakaria, T*he Future of Freedom*, pp, 205-215), from religious endogamy to unlimited "mixed marriage," from insisting on the truth of religion to stressing its practical benefits (believers live longer, etc.).

All of which is encouraging, but the campaign against God and the celebrations of his death must go on. The atheist/antitheist agenda might look something like this: First of all, rein in the intemperate unbelieving jihadis (Christopher Hitchens, Sam Harris, Michel Onfray et al.), who often get their facts wrong and constantly oversimplify the issues. Just because theists are crazy doesn't that *everything* they say is nonsense. The grand old model of unbelief—elegant, witty, accurate David Hume—is still available for copying. Writers such as Richard Dawkins and Daniel Dennett carry on the Humean tradition without resorting to journalistic overkill.

Then, the main weapon against the theists should be the "sacred" texts themselves, which surprisingly few believers really know, much less understand. The whole idea of revelation is a scoffer's dream: Your God said WHAT?! Each of the three major Scriptures, as we have seen, excels in a different kind of folly: The Old Testament has its drunken divine megalomania, the New Testament its morbid theology of atonement-through-sacrifice, and the Qur'an its paranoid hysteria. So, belly up to the bar, back to the sources. And colleges, more Bible-as-literature, please! Hire imams, where possible, to teach courses or segments of courses on the Qur'an and Islam. Expose the magniloquent frauds!

And yes, those frauds *are*—often enough—magniloquent, grandiloquent, and just plain eloquent. Look, it figures: Ever since the days of Gilgamesh, powerful, driven men have agonized over their own mortality and sought compensation-alleviation through contact with what might be called—with a sarcastic nod to crypto-atheist Matthew Arnold—that Power, not ourselves, that makes for enhanced vitality. These fancied encounters have been recorded in an often breathtaking body of work, some canonized, some not, that has been devoutly conserved, transmitted, and meditated on for millennia. Take your pick: the Book of Job,

Bach's St. Matthew Passion, Qur'an recitations by Sheikh Mustafa Ismael, whatever. It's gorgeous stuff—and, sadly, given the non-progressive nature of art, it's not going to be replaced any time soon by anything as impressive. Too bad, can't be helped. In any case, it's no use pretending that beautiful theo-fantasies (Hagia Sophia, Chartres, the Sistine Chapel, St. Paul's, etc.) are true. They aren't—even when demythologized, diluted, and served with a soupçon of philosophical relevance. For the letter kills (in more ways than one), as St. Paul warned in 2 Corinthians 3.6; but the spirit, which he thought saved the day, can't bring anything back to life; because, alas, like its supposed source, it doesn't exist. The God whom Heine described as dying has now breathed his last A-dieu.

> Though the feet of thine high priests tread
> where thy lords and our forefathers trod,
> Though these that were Gods are dead,
> and thou being dead art a God,
> Though before thee the throned Cytherean be fallen,
> and hidden her head,
> Yet thy kingdom shall pass, Galilean,
> thy dead shall go down to thee dead.
> —Swinburne, "Hymn to Proserpina"

> Here lies great Zan, whom they call Zeus.
>
> —Inscription on the tomb of Zeus in Crete

About the Author

Peter Heinegg was born in 1942 in Brooklyn to family that was one-quarter Jewish, one-half Austrian, and (thanks to a series of accidents) 100% Catholic. He attended Regis H.S. in Manhattan and entered the Jesuits in 1959, where he studied as a seminarian until 1966. He has an A.B. (English, 1965) from Fordham University and a Ph.D. (Comp. Lit., 1971) from Harvard. He has taught literature, mostly at Union College in Schenectady, N.Y., for thirty years, where he is a professor of English. He is married with two grown children. He has translated about 50 books (mostly on religion and theology) and written numerous essays, personal and otherwise, all of which may be obtained by inquiring at heineggp@union.edu. He has written *Better Than Both: The Case for Pessimism* (University Press of America, 2005); *Oh God! (And Other Follies): Essays on Religion* (UPA, 2006); and *Oh Wait—Now I Get It* (UPA, 2007).